100 favourite
&muffins
slices

Published by Hyndman Publishing,
P O Box 19, Amberley,
North Canterbury

ISBN: 1-877168-71-8

TEXT: Simon & Alison Holst

DESIGN: Dileva Design Ltd.

PHOTOGRAPHY: Lindsay Keats

PROPS: Hilary Wilson-Hill

HOME ECONOMISTS: Simon and Alison
Holst, Hilary Wilson-Hill

The recipes in this book have been carefully
tested by the authors. The publisher and the
authors have made every effort to ensure that
the instructions are accurate and safe, but they
cannot accept liability for any resulting injury or
loss or damage to property, whether direct or
consequential.

Because ovens and microwave ovens vary so
much, you should take the cooking times
suggested in recipes as guides only. The first
time you make a recipe, check it at intervals to
make sure it is not cooking faster, or more
slowly than expected.

Always follow the detailed instructions given by
manufacturers of your appliances and
equipment, rather than the more general
instructions given in these recipes.

Important Information:

For best results, use a standard metric (250ml) measuring cup
and metric measuring spoons when you use these recipes.
1 tablespoon holds 15ml.
1 teaspoon holds 5ml.

All the cup and spoon measures in the recipes are level, unless
otherwise stated. Sets of measuring cups make it easier to
measure ¼ and ½ cup quantities.

Larger amounts of butter are given by weight. Use pack
markings as a guide. Small amounts of butter are measured
using spoons (1 tablespoon of butter weighs about 15 grams).

Abbreviations used:

ml	millilitre
tsp	teaspoon
Tbsp	tablespoon
g	gram
°C	Celsius
cm	centimetre

Acknowledgements:

We would like to thank the following firms:

- **Alison's Choice:** for high quality dried fruit, fruit mixtures,
  crystallised fruit, nuts, seeds, cornmeal, chocolate chips and
  morsels which were used in all recipe development and
  photographs.

- **Benniks Poultry Farm**, Buller Road, Levin: RSPCA approved
  barn-laid eggs.

- **Goulburn Valley:** for fruit and puréed fruit (in convenient cup
  quantities) in foil topped pottles.

- **William Aitken:** for Lupi oils, grapeseed oil, and Balsamic
  vinegar.

This book contains a selection of our favourite muffin and slice
recipes. They include recipes from our books:

Marvellous Muffins
More Marvellous Muffins
Healthy & Delicious Muffins
Best Baking

For more information on these (and other titles) visit
www.hyndman.co.nz or **www.holst.co.nz**

 Recipes marked with a heart are "healthy" options. They
contain no butter, are lower in fat (especially saturated fat), and
are low cholesterol.

For tips on lowering fat and cholesterol further see page 91.

About this book

We are delighted to share with you our 100 favourite - and most popular - muffin and slice recipes. We're sure that you will enjoy making them and serving them to an appreciative audience of friends and family, as we do.

Muffins have become incredibly popular over the past few years. This is partly due to their versatility - they are much more than just useful additions to packed lunches or something to serve with coffee. It is also partly due to the fact they can be made at the drop of a hat (because they are so easy and quick to measure, mix and bake) and because they freeze and thaw so well.

As you browse through this collection you'll find muffins you can serve with a glass of juice for weekend breakfasts, with a soup, salad or sandwich for lunch, and for dessert with a cup of coffee (or even on Christmas Day, instead of mince pies). There are just so many delicious options to choose from that you should never feel you are serving "the same old thing"! We're confident that our moist and flavourful bran and/or "healthy" muffins, marked with a ♥ (which are butterless, tend to be lower in fat and contain little or virtually no saturated fat), will win over the most sceptical of tasters!

Our slices are really versatile, too. While we've tried to include plenty of "café specialities", there are also many family favourites. It's amazing how many times we heard "Ooh, my grandma used to make that…" as we put this collection together – these recipes really seem to touch a soft spot. Make a slice to add to an adult or child's packed lunch, produce one when you have a friend for coffee, or serve them for dessert – you're bound to make someone happy.

Slices don't need the skill and experience required by fancy cake recipes, but the results can be just as spectacular and memorable! Several pieces of an attractively packed slice (or a few muffins for that matter) make a great gift, too. We like the fact that many of our slices can be refrigerated for several days, or frozen for a month or two.

While you don't have to be an experienced, dedicated or wildly keen baker to have success with most of these recipes, we hope that you'll take the time to read the "Finer Points and Golden Rules" pages at the back of the book. We've been told hundreds of times that the tips and suggestions in previous books have revolutionised our readers' baking.

Have fun with our muffin and slice recipes – and enjoy the results!

Simon and Alison Holst

Contents

muffins

Best Blueberry Muffins

Everybody likes the idea of blueberry muffins. Cinnamon in the muffins themselves, and in the topping, brings out the berry flavour. Blueberries make an ideal muffin ingredient because they are not sour when cooked. Use frozen free-flow blueberries when fresh ones are not available. To stop frozen blueberries staining the batter, use them before they thaw completely.

2 cups standard (plain) flour
4 tsp baking powder
1 tsp cinnamon
½ tsp salt
¾ cup sugar

100g butter
1 cup milk
1 large egg
1–1½ cups fresh or frozen blueberries

CINNAMON SUGAR:
1 Tbsp sugar
½ tsp cinnamon

Heat oven to 220°C (210°C fanbake), with the rack just below the middle.

Sieve the first five (dry) ingredients into a fairly large bowl.

In another large bowl warm the butter until just melted, then add the milk and egg, and beat to mix thoroughly.

Prepare fresh or partly frozen berries, then tip the dry mixture and fruit into the liquids. Without overmixing (see page 90), fold everything together. Flour should be dampened, not smooth. Berries should keep their shape.

Divide the mixture evenly between 12 regular muffin pans that have been well coated with non-stick spray. Top with Cinnamon Sugar (see below) or make Streusel Topping, page 92.

Bake for 12–15 minutes, until muffins spring back when pressed. (Muffins made with frozen berries will take about 5 minutes longer.)

CINNAMON SUGAR: Mix cinnamon and sugar. Store in an airtight container until using.

YIELD: 12 regular or 24 mini muffins. **SERVE:** Always warm, for breakfast, with coffee, for lunch or for dessert.

"New Look" Blueberry Muffins

We are often told how popular our original blueberry muffins are. It was a challenge to remove the butter from the original recipe, but we're sure you will really enjoy these "new look" muffins, which contain more fruit and fibre, and almost no saturated fat.

1–1½ cups fresh or frozen blueberries
1 cup self-raising flour
¾ cup wholemeal flour
2 tsp baking powder
1 tsp cinnamon
½ tsp salt

140g pot (½ cup) apple purée
¾ cup sugar
¼ cup canola oil
1 large egg
¼ cup low-fat milk

TOPPING (OPTIONAL):
2 tsp castor sugar
½ tsp cinnamon

Heat oven to 210°C (200°C fanbake), with the rack just below the middle.

Pick over fresh blueberries or put measured, frozen berries aside to start thawing.

Mix the flours and next three ingredients into a medium-sized bowl and stir together thoroughly.

Put the next five ingredients in a large bowl and mix well. Tip in the flour mixture and fold the two mixtures together until they are fairly well combined (but do not combine completely). Add the fresh or partly thawed berries and fold through the mixture, taking care not to mix (see page 90) or break up the berries any more than necessary.

Spoon the mixture into 12 regular, thoroughly non-stick sprayed muffin pans. Sprinkle lightly with a topping made by stirring together 2 tsp castor sugar and ½ tsp cinnamon, if desired.

Bake for about 12 minutes if using fresh berries or for about 15 minutes for frozen berries. Allow to stand in their pans for 3–5 minutes, until they will lift out easily.

YIELD: 12 regular muffins. **SERVE:** As a guilt-free snack with tea or coffee, or pack in lunches. Freeze muffins which will not be used within two days.

Cinnamon & Apple Muffins

Cinnamon and apple are flavours which go wonderfully well together. Although you can use any apples you have on hand, you will get the best flavour when you choose a variety with a 'tangy' flavour such as Granny Smith, Braeburn, Sturmer or Cox's Orange.

2 medium apples (about 250g each)
1 cup low-fat plain yoghurt
¼ cup canola oil
1 large egg

1 cup sugar
1 cup wholemeal flour
1 cup standard (plain) flour
½ cup chopped walnuts
3 tsp baking powder
2 tsp cinnamon
½ tsp salt

Heat oven to 190°C (180°C fanbake), with the rack just below the middle.

Grate the unpeeled apples, discarding the cores. Place grated apple, yoghurt, oil and egg in a medium-sized bowl and mix well.

Measure all the remaining ingredients into a large bowl and stir well with a fork. Pour the liquid mixture into the dry ingredients, and gently fold together until the flour is just moistened. Do not overmix (see page 90). It doesn't matter if the mixture looks a little marbled; this looks quite good in the finished muffins.

Spray 12 regular muffin pans with non-stick spray, then divide the mixture evenly between them.

Bake for 12–15 minutes or until the muffins are golden brown on top and spring back when pressed in their centres.

Leave muffins to cool in their pans for 2–3 minutes, then tip out and cool on a rack. Place cool muffins in a plastic bag, freezing any you do not expect to eat within 48 hours.

YIELD: 12 regular muffins. **SERVE:** Warm, any time, with tea or coffee, or include in packed lunches as a guiltless treat. Good topped with cottage cheese.

Fabulous Feijoa Muffins

Why are these muffins fabulous? Well, even people who do not like feijoas keep reaching for yet another! The added orange rind and juice, and a cinnamon topping make the muffins really interesting, without overwhelming the feijoa flavour.

75g butter, melted
1 cup finely chopped feijoa flesh
2 large eggs
finely grated rind of 1 orange
¼ cup orange juice

¾ cup sugar
2 cups self-raising flour

1 tsp cinnamon
1 Tbsp sugar

Heat oven to 210°C (200°C fanbake), with the rack just below the middle.

Heat the butter in a large bowl until it is liquid. Halve the feijoas and scoop out the central part with a teaspoon. (Muffins are nicest if you do not use much of the firmer outer shell.) Chop feijoa into pieces no bigger than peas. Pack into cup measure, then mix this into the melted butter with a fork.

Add the unbeaten eggs, orange rind, and the juice of the orange (made up to volume with a little lemon juice if necessary). Mix until everything is combined.

Mix the sugar and self-raising flour in another container. Sprinkle it over the egg mixture, then fold it in without overmixing. (If you have used too much firm feijoa flesh you may need to add a little extra juice or milk to reach usual muffin consistency.)

Divide the mixture between 12 regular or 24 mini muffin pans which have been lightly buttered or non-stick sprayed. Mix the cinnamon and second measure of sugar, and sprinkle it on the muffins.

Bake for 10–15 minutes, until the centres spring back when pressed.

VARIATION: For Raspberry and Feijoa Muffins, add an extra ¼ cup of sugar and fold in 1 cup of frozen raspberries.

YIELD: 12 regular or 24 mini muffins. **SERVE:** Slightly warm for best flavour, at any time of day.

Cranberry & Apple Muffins

By adding fruit purée to uncooked muffin mixture, you can produce tender, moist muffins using the minimum amount of oil or butter. We have added dried cranberries as well, for their tartness, but you can replace them with sultanas or raisins if you prefer these.

½ cup (60g) dried cranberries (often called "craisins")
½ cup boiling water
140g pot (½ cup) apple purée
½ cup canola or other oil
1 large egg
¼–½ cup chopped walnuts (optional)

1 cup self-raising flour
¾ cup wholemeal flour
¾ cup sugar
2 tsp baking powder
½ tsp salt

Heat oven to 210°C (200°C fanbake), with the rack just below the middle.

Pour the boiling water over the dried cranberries and leave them to stand for about 5 minutes. Without draining, add the apple purée, the oil and the egg, and mix well with a fork. Stir in the chopped nuts if you are adding them.

Measure the flours into another bowl. Add the remaining dry ingredients, and mix with a fork or whisk.

Sprinkle this mixture over the liquid ingredients and fold them together, stopping as soon as there are no pockets or streaks of flour. Do not overmix (see page 90).

Spoon the mixture into 12 regular, thoroughly non-stick sprayed muffin pans.

Bake for 10–12 minutes, until lightly browned, and until the centres spring back when pressed. Stand in their pans for 2–4 minutes, or until the muffins may be lifted out without breaking them.

VARIATION: For Sultana and Apple Muffins, replace the cranberries with sultanas. Pour boiling water over them and proceed in the same way.

YIELD: 12 regular-sized muffins. **SERVE:** Plain or dusted with icing sugar, at any time of day with tea or coffee.

Spiced Apple Muffins

Make these muffins only after you know what consistency a muffin mixture should be when the dry ingredients are combined with the wet ingredients. Raw apple gives muffins a lovely fresh flavour, but when you use it, you never know exactly how much milk will be needed as well.

1 cup self-raising flour
1 cup (fine) rolled oats
¾ cup brown sugar
2 tsp mixed spice
2 tsp cinnamon
½ tsp ground cloves
½ tsp baking soda
½ tsp salt

75g butter
1 large egg
¾–1 cup milk
1 cup raw chopped or grated apple

Heat oven to 200°C (190°C fanbake), with the rack just below the middle.

Measure the dry ingredients into a large mixing bowl and mix well with your fingers to ensure that the rolled oats and brown sugar are mixed evenly through the other ingredients.

Melt the butter in another large bowl, then add the egg and ¾ cup of the milk, and beat with a fork until mixed.

Next, grate or chop the apple in a food processor. Press it into the cup, removing air bubbles, then stir it into the liquids. (Work quickly to prevent the apple browning.)

Sprinkle the dry ingredients onto the apple-liquid mixture, then fold in to barely dampen the dry ingredients (see page 90), adding as much of the extra ¼ cup of milk as you need.

Coat 12 regular muffin pans with non-stick spray and divide the mixture between them.

Bake for 12–15 minutes or until the muffins spring back when pressed. Leave for 3–4 minutes before removing from the pans and cooling on a wire rack.

YIELD: 12 regular or 24 mini muffins. **SERVE:** For morning tea or brunch. Nice in packed lunches and popular as after school snacks.

Glazed Passionfruit Muffins

These muffins are a special treat for lucky people growing their own purple (or black) passionfruit, or those with a friend who grows enough passionfruit to share! (Freeze unsweetened pulp so you can make these muffins out of season, too.)

50g butter, melted
½ cup sour cream
¼–½ cup fresh passionfruit pulp
up to ¼ cup orange juice
2 large eggs
¾ cup sugar
2 cups self-raising flour

2 Tbsp passionfruit pulp
¼ cup icing sugar

Heat oven to 210°C (200°C fanbake), with the rack just below the middle.

Melt the butter in a large bowl, then stir in the sour cream. Halve the passionfruit and scoop out all the pulp with a teaspoon. (Put aside two tablespoons to make the glaze.) You need at least ¼ cup to get a good flavour. Make it up to ½ cup with orange juice if necessary. Add to the bowl. Break the eggs into the bowl, add the sugar, then beat with a fork until well blended.

Sprinkle or sieve the flour onto the mixture in the bowl, then fold it in, taking care not to overmix (see page 90). Divide the mixture between 12 regular or 24 mini muffin pans which have been thoroughly coated with non-stick spray.

Bake for 10–15 minutes, until tops spring back when pressed.

While muffins cook, mix the reserved passionfruit pulp and the icing sugar to a pouring consistency. Spoon or brush it over the muffins as soon as you take them from the oven.

YIELD: 12 regular or 24 mini muffins. **SERVE:** Preferably on the day they are made, cold or slightly warm, unbuttered, with tea or coffee.

Apricot & Walnut Muffins

Dried fruits and nuts always make good additions to muffins! If you can find New Zealand dried apricots, use them in this recipe; they break up easily after being heated in the water or juice, giving an extra-strong apricot flavour to the mixture.

2 cups standard (plain) flour
1 tsp baking soda
1 cup brown sugar
1 tsp cinnamon

½ cup chopped dried apricots
¼ cup water or orange juice

100g butter
2 large eggs
1 cup plain or apricot yoghurt
1 large orange, rind and juice
½ cup chopped walnuts

Heat oven to 190°C (180°C fanbake), with the rack just below the middle.

Measure the dry ingredients into a large bowl and mix well to ensure that the brown sugar is evenly mixed through the other ingredients.

In another bowl microwave the apricots with the water or juice until all the liquid is absorbed (about 1 minute on High (100%) power).

Add the butter, warming again if necessary, then mix in the eggs and yoghurt, and the grated rind. Make the juice from the orange up to ½ cup with water, if necessary, and add this and the chopped walnuts to the egg mixture.

Tip the dry ingredients into the liquids, then gently fold the two mixtures together, taking care not to overmix (see page 90). Divide the mixture evenly between 12 regular muffin pans that have been well coated with non-stick spray.

Bake for about 12–15 minutes or until the muffins spring back when pressed lightly.

YIELD: 12 regular or 24 mini muffins. **SERVE:** For a weekend brunch, or with coffee any time. Good in packed lunches, for after school snacks and for picnics.

Upside-Down Nectarine Muffins

These are delicious in summer made with fresh, locally grown fruit, but try making them with Californian nectarines when you have the midwinter blues – the smell as they bake just seems to fill the house with sunshine!

12 tsp (about 50g) butter or oil
½ cup brown sugar
3 nectarines

2 cups self-raising flour
¾ cup sugar
1 tsp mixed spice
¾ tsp salt

2 large eggs
¾ cup plain or apricot yoghurt
¼ cup canola or other oil
1 tsp vanilla

Heat oven to 200°C (190°C fanbake), with the rack just below the middle.

Non-stick spray 12 regular muffin pans. Put a teaspoon of butter in each pan and place the pans in the oven until the butter melts, or use oil. Remove from the oven and sprinkle 2 teaspoons of brown sugar evenly over the bottom of each pan. Quarter the nectarines and cut each quarter into three slices. Arrange three slices on top of the butter-sugar mixture in each pan.

Measure the dry ingredients into a large bowl and stir to combine.

In another large bowl lightly beat together the eggs, yoghurt, oil and vanilla.

Sprinkle the flour mixture over the liquids and fold gently together, stopping as soon as the flour is moistened (see page 90). Spoon the batter into the nectarine-lined pans.

Bake for 12–15 minutes until golden brown. (Muffins may be flat topped – this is not a problem! Muffin pans may need soaking later.)

After 2 minutes standing, press down gently on each muffin and rotate about ½ a turn, then lift the muffins onto a rack. The topping usually lifts off with the muffin if you get it at the right stage – not too soon, and not too late. Reposition any fruit that stays in the pans.

YIELD: 12 regular muffins. **SERVE:** Warm or reheated, within a few hours of cooking. Suitable for any meal, from breakfast to dessert.

Rich Raspberry Muffins

These muffins combine the flavours of raspberries and spices. You will find the same popular ingredients in Belgium biscuits and in Linzer Torte - but it takes a long time to prepare these. Do it the easy way – enjoy the same flavours in quickly-made muffins!

2 cups self-raising flour
½ cup sugar
1 tsp cinnamon
¼ tsp ground cloves

100g butter
1 tsp instant coffee
1 cup milk
1 large egg
rind of 1 lemon
½ cup raspberry jam*

* Use homemade jam if possible, since this usually has a stronger raspberry flavour. If not available, use good quality "bought" jam.

Heat oven to 200°C (190°C fanbake), with the rack just below the middle.

Sift the dry ingredients into a large bowl.

Melt the butter in another bowl. Dissolve the instant coffee in the milk, then add to the melted butter along with the egg. Add the lemon rind and mix well to combine.

Sprinkle the dry ingredients over the liquids, then fold together without overmixing (see page 90).

Coat 12 regular muffin pans with non-stick spray. Half fill each pan with the muffin mixture, then make a small depression on the surface of each one with a damp teaspoon. Put 2 teaspoons of the jam in each depression, then spoon the remaining mixture over the filling, taking care to cover it completely.

Bake for 10–12 minutes or until the centres spring back when lightly pressed. Leave to stand in the pans for about 3 minutes before removing to a wire rack. Before muffins cool completely, drizzle with a small amount of the icing made by combining ¼ cup of sifted icing sugar with just enough lemon juice (1-2 tsp) to mix to the consistency of thin cream.

YIELD: 12 regular muffins. **SERVE:** With tea, coffee or for dessert.

Spicy Pineapple Muffins

These muffins are deliciously spicy. They freeze well and can be thawed in a warm oven in 5–10 minutes. The quantity of mixed spice really is 1 tablespoon, but remember to use a level measure.

2 cups standard (plain) flour
1 Tbsp mixed spice
1 tsp baking soda
½ cup sugar
¼ tsp salt
1 cup sultanas

100g butter
2 large eggs
450g can crushed pineapple

Heat oven to 200°C (190°C fanbake), with the rack just below the middle.

Sieve into a large bowl the flour, mixed spice, baking soda, sugar and salt. Add the sultanas and toss with the flour mixture to combine.

Melt the butter in another large bowl. Add the eggs and beat well. Drain the pineapple through a sieve, pushing with a spoon to extract as much liquid as possible. Measure the drained pineapple to ensure you have about 1 cup of fruit and ¾ cup juice. Add the measured fruit and juice to the egg mixture.

Tip the dry ingredients over the liquid mixture, then fold everything together until the flour has been dampened, but the mixture still looks lumpy and undermixed (see page 90).

Spray 12 regular muffin pans with non-stick spray. Put about ¼ cup of mixture into each muffin cup.

Bake for 10–15 minutes, until muffins spring back when pressed in the centre.

YIELD: 12 regular muffins. **SERVE:** Warm with morning or afternoon tea, in a packed lunch, or when it is your turn to "bring a plate".

Rum & Raisin Muffins

We make these muffins for a cold weather treat. If you're going to serve them with coffee or for lunch, try drizzling them with a rum flavoured glaze. If they are for dessert or supper, reheat them in the microwave and serve them with rum butter (see page 92) for a real treat!

1 cup dark Californian raisins
2 Tbsp rum

2 cups standard (plain) flour
1½ tsp baking soda
2 tsp cinnamon
2 tsp mixed spice
¼ tsp ground cloves
¾ cup sugar
½ cup chopped walnuts

75g butter
1 large egg
1 cup yoghurt (any flavour)
¾ cup milk

Heat oven to 210°C (200°C fanbake), with the rack just below the middle.

Put the raisins and rum into a small plastic bag. Knead bag gently. Leave to stand in a warm place while you mix the other ingredients.

Sieve the flour, soda and spices into a large bowl. Add the sugar and chopped walnuts and stir to mix thoroughly.

Melt the butter in a pot or microwave dish. Add the egg, yoghurt (any flavour) and milk. Add the marinated raisins with any remaining liquid and mix well. Now combine the liquid and dry mixtures without overmixing (see page 90).

Divide the mixture evenly between 12 regular muffin pans that have been well coated with non-stick spray.

Bake for about 12 minutes or until the centres spring back when pressed. Leave to stand in the pans for about 3 minutes before removing and cooling on a wire rack.

TO GLAZE: Mix ¼ cup icing sugar with ½ teaspoon rum essence and about 1–2 teaspoon/s milk to make a thin icing. Drizzle, in a thin stream, over warm muffins on rack.

YIELD: 12 regular or 24 mini muffins. **SERVE:** For holiday season brunches, with coffee in mid-winter, or for dessert with rum butter on any occasion.

Carrot & Pineapple Muffins

After you've made these once, you'll find you need to keep a small can of pineapple on hand so that you can make them at any time. They're so good the requests just keep coming!

2 cups wholemeal flour
4 tsp baking powder
¾ cup brown sugar
2 tsp cinnamon
1 tsp mixed spice
½–1 tsp salt
½ cup chopped walnuts

1 150g carrot, grated (1 cup)
1 small (227g) can crushed
   pineapple
¼ cup orange juice
1 large egg
¼ cup canola oil or 50g butter

Heat oven to 200°C (190°C fanbake), with the rack just below the middle.

Measure the first seven ingredients into a large bowl. Use the larger amount of salt if you are going to use oil rather than butter. Mix well using your hands, making sure that there are no large lumps of sugar in the mixture.

Grate the carrot. (If you are not sure of the quantity, weigh the carrot before grating it, or pack the grated carrot firmly into a cup measure.) Mix the grated carrot, the contents of the can of crushed pineapple (fruit and juice), orange juice, egg and oil or melted butter together in another large bowl.

Tip the dry mixture into the liquid and fold everything together, until the flour is just moistened. Take care to avoid overmixing (see page 90). Add a little extra juice if the mixture seems thicker than usual.

Spoon the mixture into 12 regular or 24 mini muffin pans, that have been lightly buttered or non-stick sprayed.

Bake for 12–15 minutes, or until the muffins spring back when pressed in the middle.

OPTIONAL: As soon as you have taken the muffins from their pans, brush all their surfaces with a mixture of ¼ cup each of lemon juice and sugar.

YIELD: 12 regular muffins or 24 mini muffins. **SERVE:** Extra good straight from the oven or reheated. Pack frozen mini muffins in children's lunch boxes.

♥ Carrot & Walnut Muffins

If you like the flavour of hot cross buns but don't have the time to make them, try these spicy muffins instead. Don't save them only for Easter celebrations though – they taste good at any time.

1½ cups standard (plain) flour
½ tsp salt
¾ tsp baking soda
2 tsp cinnamon
1 tsp ground allspice
¾ cup brown sugar
¼ cup chopped walnuts
½ cup sultanas

½ cup canola or other oil
2 large eggs
200g carrots, grated

Heat oven to 190°C (180°C fanbake), with the rack just below the middle.

Sieve the first five ingredients into a large bowl. Add brown sugar, walnuts and sultanas and mix these evenly through the dry ingredients with your fingers, breaking up any lumps.

Beat the oil and eggs together in another bowl, then add the finely grated carrot.

Tip the dry mixture into the wet ingredients and fold everything together until there are no more unmixed lumps of flour. Take care not to overmix (see page 90).

Spray 12 regular muffin pans with non-stick spray. Put about ¼ cup of mixture into each pan.

Bake for about 15 minutes, or until the centres of the muffins spring back when pressed.

YIELD: 12 regular or 24 mini muffins. **SERVE:** Warm with coffee. Nice for dessert, split in half and spread with rum butter (see page 92).

Raspberry & White Chocolate Muffins

These muffins have a zingy raspberry flavour which goes very nicely with the hint of vanilla provided by a little white chocolate. If you don't like the idea of chocolate in low-fat muffins, try replacing it with the same quantity of chopped macadamia nuts.

1 cup (150g) frozen raspberries
1 cup (2 x 150g pots) extra low-fat (2%) sour cream
½ cup low-fat milk
¼ cup canola oil
1 large egg
1 tsp vanilla

2 cups self-raising flour
1 cup sugar
¼ cup white chocolate morsels
½ tsp baking soda
½ tsp salt

Heat oven to 190°C (180°C fanbake), with the rack just below the middle.

Measure the raspberries into a large bowl and leave to soften for a few minutes. Add the sour cream, milk, oil, egg and vanilla to the bowl and stir well so the raspberries break up a little. (The berries don't have to be mashed, but whole berries are quite large.)

Tip the flour, sugar, chocolate morsels, baking soda and salt into another bowl and stir them together well with a whisk or fork.

Sprinkle the dry ingredients into the liquid mixture, then stir until the flour is just moistened. Do not overmix (see page 90). This is quite a wet looking mixture, but this doesn't seem to matter in the end.

Spoon the mixture into 12 regular, non-stick sprayed muffin pans.

Bake for 15–18 minutes, until golden brown and a skewer comes out clean. (The frozen raspberries cool the mixture down, so these muffins do tend to take a little longer to cook.)

Remove the muffins from the oven and leave to cool in their pans for 2–3 minutes before cooling on a rack.

YIELD: 12 regular muffins. **SERVE:** Enjoy warm, or cool then store in a plastic bag. The raspberry flavour actually improves with standing.

Double Chocolate Surprise Muffins

I invented this recipe for my little chocolate book, but it is too good to leave out of this muffin collection. Make it without the raspberry "surprise" if you like, but it won't be quite as good.

1¾ cups standard (plain) flour
4 tsp baking powder
¼ cup cocoa
½ cup sugar
½ cup (100g) chocolate chips

75g butter, melted
2 large eggs
¾ cup milk
¾–1 cup raspberry jam
extra chocolate chips

Heat oven to 200°C (190°C fanbake), with the rack just below the middle.

Sift the flour, baking powder and cocoa together into a medium-sized bowl. Add the sugar and chocolate chips and toss with a fork to mix.

Melt the butter in a large bowl until just liquid, then add the eggs and milk and beat with a fork until well combined and smooth. Sprinkle the flour mixture over the liquids and fold together, mixing as little as possible. Stop as soon as there are no pockets of flour left, as overmixing spoils muffins (see page 90).

Coat 12 regular muffin pans lightly with non-stick spray or butter, then half fill each pan by spooning about a tablespoon of the mixture into the prepared pans, using two spoons.

Using a damp teaspoon make a small hollow in each muffin and fill it with a teaspoon of jam. Divide the remaining mixture between the muffins, ensuring that the jam is completely covered. Sprinkle each with a few extra chocolate chips if desired.

Bake for about 10 minutes or until the centres spring back when pressed. Leave to stand for several minutes before twisting and removing from the pans. Leave to cool on a rack.

YIELD: 12 regular muffins. **SERVE:** Best enjoyed warm. For a quick dessert serve with lightly whipped cream.

Chocolate & Banana Muffins

Here is a recipe which is well worth trying. The banana flavour is strongest when you use over-ripe bananas. If you do not like the idea of pieces of chocolate in muffins, replace the chocolate with half the amount of chopped walnuts.

2 cups self-raising flour
½ cup castor sugar
½ cup chocolate chips
½ tsp salt

100g butter
1 cup milk
1 large egg
1 tsp vanilla
1 cup (2–3) mashed bananas

Heat oven to 220°C (210°C fanbake), with the rack just below the middle.

With a fork, stir the flour, castor sugar, chocolate chips and salt together in a large bowl.

Melt the butter in another large bowl, remove from the heat, then add the milk, egg and vanilla and beat well.

Mash and measure the bananas, then stir them into the liquid. Tip all the flour mixture into the bowl with the liquid mixture. Fold everything together carefully until all the flour is dampened, stopping before the mixture is smooth (see page 90).

Spray 12 regular muffin pans with non-stick spray. Put about ¼ cup of mixture into each cup.

Bake for 12–15 minutes, until muffins spring back when pressed in the centre.

YIELD: 12 regular or 24 mini muffins. **SERVE:** Mini muffins make very popular snacks for young children, and are good for lunch boxes and after school snacks. Serve with tea or coffee at any time of the day.

♥ A B C Muffins

A is for apple, B is for banana, C is for chocolate! We usually make these in mini muffin pans and freeze a good proportion of them, because they will thaw quickly in lunch boxes or spur-of-the-moment picnic packs. We find that it is not only children who enjoy mini muffins!

1 cup (2–3) mashed ripe bananas
½ cup brown sugar
¼ tsp salt
¼ cup canola oil
1 large egg
½ cup low-fat milk
¼–½ cup chocolate chips
1 apple*, grated or finely chopped
2 cups self-raising flour

* Use a "tangy" apple such as Braeburn, Cox's Orange, Sturmer or Granny Smith for best flavour.

Heat oven to 210°C (200°C fanbake), with the rack just below the middle.

Mash the ripe bananas on a board using a fork. In a large bowl, mix together the mashed banana, sugar, salt, oil, egg and milk until well mixed. Stir in the chocolate chips and the unpeeled apple which has been coarsely grated or chopped in a food processor.

Stir the flour in its container, then spoon it into the cup measure without packing it or banging it down. Sprinkle it over the top of the other ingredients, then fold it in without overmixing, stopping when there are no streaks or pockets of flour visible (see page 90).

Spoon into mini muffin pans (or regular muffin pans) which have been thoroughly sprayed with non-stick spray.

Bake for 10–12 minutes or until golden brown, and until the tops spring back when pressed lightly. Leave to stand 2–3 minutes in their pans, then remove carefully and cool on a rack. If making these for adults, coat with crunchy lemon glaze.

CRUNCHY LEMON GLAZE: While muffins cool in pans, mix 2 tablespoons each of lemon juice and sugar. Transfer muffins from pans to a rack and immediately brush with the lemon mixture, making sure that some undissolved sugar is on each muffin.

YIELD: 24 mini or 12 regular muffins. **SERVE:** Any time as a healthy snack. Store in plastic bags when cold, freezing muffins which will not be eaten in 2 days.

Macadamia & White Chocolate Muffins

These "All White" or "White Christmas" muffins are rich and "cakey" with a delicious vanilla flavour. They may look plain on the outside, but inside they are full of chunky pieces of white chocolate and macadamia.

2 cups standard (plain) flour
3 tsp baking powder
1 cup sugar
½ cup (75g) chopped macadamia nuts
¾ cup (100g) chopped white chocolate

100g butter
1 cup milk
1 large egg
2 tsp vanilla

Heat oven to 200°C (190°C fanbake), with the rack just below the middle.

Measure the flour, baking powder and sugar into a large bowl. Add the chopped macadamia nuts and chopped white chocolate, then mix well with a fork to combine.

Melt the butter in another large bowl, then add the milk, egg and vanilla and beat with the fork until thoroughly blended.

Tip the flour mixture into the liquid and gently fold together until the flour is moistened. Do not overmix (see page 90).

Spoon the batter into 12 non-stick sprayed or lightly buttered, regular muffin pans, or 24 mini muffin pans.

Bake for about 12 minutes until golden brown, and firm when pressed in the centre.

NOTE: We used roasted, salted macadamia nuts (which we had bought for nibbling) when we made these. They were excellent for both purposes!

YIELD: 12 regular or 24 mini muffins. **SERVE:** Only slightly warm or cold (definitely unbuttered), with coffee or for dessert. Great for gifts.

Christmas Mincemeat Muffins

Although mincemeat pies are nice, making their crust is quite time consuming, especially when there are other Christmas chores waiting. Why not put spoonfuls of the mixture in muffins instead? Serve these warm, and wait for the compliments!

1¾ cups self-raising flour
¾ cup castor sugar
½ tsp salt

2 large eggs
½ cup sour cream
½ cup milk
½ tsp rum, whisky or brandy essence
½ cup Christmas (fruit) mincemeat

Heat oven to 200°C (190°C fanbake), with the rack just below the middle.

Measure the first three ingredients into a bowl and mix together with a fork or whisk. In another large bowl, whisk the eggs, sour cream, milk and essence of your choice together until smooth. Add the dry ingredients to the liquids and, without overmixing (see page 90), stir gently to combine.

Coat 12 regular muffin pans with non-stick spray and half fill the 12 pans with the mixture. Using a dampened teaspoon, make a small indentation on the top of each, and into it put 1–2 teaspoons of the mincemeat. Cover each with a spoonful of the remaining mixture, trying to cover the "enclosed" mincemeat.

Bake for about 12–15 minutes or until golden brown. The centres should spring back when pressed. Cool in the pans for 3–4 minutes before removing to a rack.

YIELD: 12 regular muffins. **SERVE:** Best warm, ideal for Christmas Day breakfast or brunch, or with coffee at any time of the day over the holiday period. Serve hot for dessert between Christmas and New Year, with fresh berries and ice-cream or whipped cream, or rum butter (see page 92).

Moist Chocolate Muffins

These muffins are so moist and delicious it's hard to believe that they're actually pretty low in fat. If you really want to lower the fat content even further, you can omit the chocolate chips, but there are in fact only 1 teaspoonful of them per (regular-sized) muffin, so it really is a case of a little going a long way…

1 cup (about 200g) pitted prunes
½ cup boiling water
½ cup cold water
½ cup (150g) extra low-fat (2%) sour cream
¼ cup canola oil
1 large egg
1½ tsp lecithin (optional)

1¾ cups standard (plain) flour
½ cup sugar
¼ cup cocoa powder
4 tsp baking powder
½ tsp salt
¼ cup chocolate chips (optional)

Heat oven to 190°C (180°C fanbake), with the rack just below the middle.

Place the prunes in a food processor and add the boiling water. Process until the prunes are well chopped, then add the next 4 ingredients (or 5 if using the lecithin) and process until the mixture is smooth and creamy.

Measure the remaining dry ingredients, including the chocolate chips (if using), into a large bowl and toss together until well mixed.

Pour the liquid ingredients into the dry mixture, and fold together gently, stirring no more than is absolutely necessary (see page 90).

Spoon the mixture into 12 regular (or 24 mini) non-stick sprayed, muffin pans.

Bake for 12–15 minutes until centres spring back when pressed lightly. Remember that mini muffins will cook more quickly than larger muffins.

Remove from the oven and leave to cool in the pans for 2-3 minutes until the muffins will come out cleanly.

YIELD: 12 regular or 24 mini muffins. **SERVE:** As is, or dusted lightly with icing sugar.

Double Chocolate Muffins

This recipe will delight chocolate lovers! You might think that chocolate chips on top of a chocolate muffin is 'gilding the lily', but they provide an interesting texture, and add intensity to the flavour.

1¾ cups standard (plain) flour
1 tsp baking soda
1 cup castor sugar
¼ cup cocoa

100g butter
1 large egg
1 cup plain or raspberry yoghurt
½ cup milk
½ tsp vanilla

¼–½ cup chocolate chips

Heat oven to 200°C (190°C fanbake), with the rack just below the middle.

Sift the dry ingredients into a large mixing bowl.

Melt the butter in another large bowl, then add the next four ingredients and mix until smooth.

Sprinkle the flour mixture over the liquids, and fold together until the flour is dampened, but not smooth. Divide the mixture evenly between 12 regular muffin pans that have been well coated with non-stick spray (particularly important if using the chocolate chips).

If desired, sprinkle the top of each muffin with 1–2 tsp chocolate chips before baking.

Bake for 10–12 minutes or until centres spring back when pressed lightly. Leave to stand in the pans for about 3 minutes before removing and cooling on a wire rack.

YIELD: 12 regular or 24 mini muffins. **SERVE:** With coffee for lunch. Make mini muffins for children's parties. Split muffins and serve for dessert with fresh strawberries or with raspberry jam and whipped cream.

Wheat-Free Double Chocolate Muffins

These wheat-free muffins make a treat for anybody who cannot eat a chocolate cake made with flour, and will be enjoyed by everyone in the family. They can be "dressed up" for a party, too.

1 cup rice flour
¼ cup cocoa powder
½ tsp baking soda
½ tsp salt
1 cup castor sugar

2 large eggs, separated
1 cup plain or fruit flavoured yoghurt
½ cup chocolate chips

Heat oven to 200°C (190°C fanbake), with the rack just below the middle.

Sift the rice flour, cocoa, baking soda and salt and half of the sugar into a large bowl.

Separate the eggs, putting the whites into a large clean glass or metal bowl, and mixing the yolks with the yoghurt in another container.

Using an electric (or hand) beater, beat the egg whites until their peaks turn over when the beater is lifted from them, then add the remaining sugar and continue to beat until they will again form peaks that turn over.

Stir the egg yolk and yoghurt mixture into the dry ingredients, then fold in a third of the beaten egg whites. Gently fold in the remaining egg whites and the chocolate chips. This should make a very soft, light batter.

Spoon the batter into 12 regular muffin pans which have been thoroughly non-stick sprayed or oiled.

Bake for 12-15 minutes until firm when pressed in the centre. Stand in the pans for 3-4 minutes before removing and cooling on a rack.

YIELD: 12 regular, slightly compact muffins. **SERVE:** Warm or cold. Cut out centres and fill with whipped cream for "fairy cakes" for wheat-free diets, if desired.

Wheat-Free Blueberry Muffins

Somewhere along the line, blueberry muffins seem to have become the 'standard' sweet muffin, so we decided they were the ideal candidate for a 'wheat-free make-over'. Because the rice flour seems to 'set' at room temperature, these are best served warm from the oven or reheated.

1 cup brown sugar
½ cup canola oil
2 large eggs
1¼ cups plain or fruit flavoured unsweetened yoghurt
1 tsp vanilla
¼ tsp salt
1 cup fine cornmeal
1 cup rice flour
3 tsp wheat-free baking powder
1 tsp cinnamon
1 cup fresh or frozen blueberries

Heat the oven to 200°C (190°C fanbake), with the rack just below the middle.

Measure the sugar and oil into a food processor, and process until smooth. Add the eggs and process again until the mixture is light and creamy looking.

Pour in the yoghurt and vanilla, then sprinkle in the salt. Process until mixed.

Measure in the cornmeal, rice flour, baking powder and cinnamon, then process in short bursts until there are no lumps. Remove the processor blade, then add the blueberries and stir by hand just enough to mix them evenly through.

Thoroughly non-stick spray 12 regular muffin pans, then divide the mixture evenly between them using two large spoons.

Bake for 12–15 minutes, or until golden brown. Remove from the oven and leave to stand for 3–4 minutes before removing from the pans.

YIELD: 12 regular muffins (regular are best for these, as mini muffins tend to get a little dry). **SERVE:** Best enjoyed warm from the oven or reheated.

♥ Apricot Surprise Muffins

These muffins are one of Alison's favourites. When you bite into them, you find a delicious mixture of dried apricots and almonds hidden in the middle. Make them for special occasions or for your best friends – but make sure you keep some for yourself!

1¾ cups self-raising flour
¾ cup sugar
¼ tsp baking soda
½ tsp salt

½ cup extra low-fat (2%) sour cream
½ cup milk
1 large egg
½ tsp almond essence

50g dried apricots
½ cup water
2 Tbsp ground almonds
2 Tbsp sugar
2 Tbsp Wine biscuit crumbs

Heat oven to 200°C (190°C fanbake), with the rack just below the middle.

Measure the first 4 (dry) ingredients into a bowl and mix thoroughly.

Beat the sour cream, milk, egg and almond essence together in a large bowl. Tip the flour mixture into the liquids, then fold everything together, taking care not to overmix (see page 90).

To make the filling, chop the apricots into small pieces. Boil them with the water for 3-4 minutes, until the water has disappeared. Cool, and mix with the ground almonds, sugar and biscuit crumbs.

Spray 12 regular muffin pans with non-stick spray. Half fill each one with the muffin mixture. Make a small depression on the surface of each one with a damp teaspoon. Divide the apricot filling mixture between the 12 cups and place carefully in the depression. Spoon the remaining mixture over the filling, taking care to cover it completely.

Optional, but very nice: Sprinkle with Streusel Topping (see page 92).

Bake for 12–15 minutes, until muffins spring back when pressed.

YIELD: 12 regular or 24 mini muffins. **SERVE:** Warm with coffee, or with whipped cream as a dessert.

Fruit Salad Muffins

When you want to brighten a winter's day and you don't have fresh fruit on hand, drain a can of fruit salad and use it, and some of the juice from it, to make these fruit salad muffins!

2 cups standard (plain) flour
4 tsp baking powder
½ cup sugar
½ tsp salt

425g can Fruit Salad
75g butter
½ cup milk
1 large egg

OPTIONAL TOPPING:

1 Tbsp sugar
½ tsp cinnamon

Heat oven to 200°C (190°C fanbake), with the rack just below the middle.

Sift the flour, baking powder, sugar and salt together into a large mixing bowl.

Drain (and reserve) the juice from the can of fruit salad. Measure ¼ cup of this juice and add to the melted butter with the milk and egg in another large bowl. Beat with a whisk or fork to combine.

Cut any large pieces of fruit (and the cherries) into smaller pieces. Add the fruit and the sifted dry ingredients to the liquids, then mix briefly, until just combined (see page 90).

Coat 12 regular muffin pans with non-stick spray and spoon about ¼ cup of the mixture into each pan.

Make the topping by mixing together the second measure of sugar and the cinnamon, and sprinkle over the top of each of the muffins.

Bake for 10–12 minutes or until the centres spring back when pressed. Leave to stand in the pans for about 3 minutes before removing and cooling on a wire rack.

YIELD: 12 regular or 24 mini muffins. **SERVE:** Warm or cold for weekend breakfast or brunch, with tea or coffee at any time of day, or for dessert.

Coconut, Cherry & Cream Cheese Muffins ▶

Coconut cakes have long been popular in our family. Perhaps the most popular was a coconut and cherry cake, and it was really only a matter of time before we applied this theme to muffins.

1½ cups standard (plain) flour
1 cup sugar
3 tsp baking powder
½ tsp salt
1 cup fine desiccated coconut

½ cup cream cheese
¾ cup milk
1 large egg
1 tsp vanilla
¼ tsp almond essence
½–1 cup (150g) glacé cherries, halved
shredded coconut to decorate (optional)

Heat oven to 200°C (190°C fanbake), with the rack just below the middle.

Sift the flour, sugar, baking powder and salt into a large bowl. Add the grated coconut and toss together.

Soften the cream cheese by warming it first, then place it in a large bowl and beat it together with the milk, egg and essences.

Sprinkle the dry ingredients over the liquid mixture, add the cherries, then gently fold everything together, stopping as soon as all the flour is moistened (see page 90).

Spoon the mixture into 12 regular non-stick sprayed muffin pans. Sprinkle with some long shreds of coconut if you have it.

Bake for 12 minutes, or until golden brown and firm when pressed in the centre.

YIELD: 12 regular muffins. **SERVE:** Good cold or slightly warm, within two days of making.

♥ Tutti Fruity Muffins

These low-fat muffins are always popular. They have such a good flavour they do not need buttering, as long as you eat them warm from the oven. Like any low-fat baking, they stale quickly, so if you are not going to eat them all the day they are made, you should freeze those which are left.

2 cups standard (plain) flour
1 cup oat bran
1 tsp baking soda
1 tsp baking powder
1 cup brown sugar

2 large eggs
¾ cup apricot or orange yoghurt
½ cup milk
¼ cup concentrated orange juice
1 banana, mashed
2 Tbsp passionfruit pulp, if available

Heat oven to 200°C (190°C fanbake), with the rack just below the middle.

Toss the flour, oat bran, baking soda and baking powder together, thoroughly, in a large mixing bowl. Add the sugar and mix again.

In another large bowl, beat the eggs, yoghurt, milk and orange juice together, using a fork. Add the mashed banana (and passionfruit, if using) and mix again.

Tip the dry ingredients into the liquid mixture, then fold the two together, stopping as soon as the dry ingredients are dampened. Take care not to overmix (see page 90).

Put spoonfuls of the mixture into 12 regular muffin pans that have been thoroughly coated with non-stick spray.

Bake for 10–15 minutes or until the centres spring back when pressed.

YIELD: 12 regular or 24 mini muffins. **SERVE:** For breakfasts, brunches, as after school snacks, for picnics and in packed lunches, within 36 hours.

Mango & Orange Muffins

These muffins have a pleasantly gentle mango-and-orange background flavour and colour. We enjoy them with coffee at any time of day, finding that a few muffins from the freezer are particularly useful for a quick dessert.

½ cup (65g) finely chopped dried
    mango slices*
½ cup orange and mango juice (or
    orange juice)

1 cup plain low-fat yoghurt, or
    orange or mango yoghurt
¼ cup canola or other oil
1 large egg
1 tsp vanilla
½ tsp salt

2 cups self-raising flour
1 cup sugar

* We used Alison's Choice self-select dried
  mango slices, available from larger New
  World supermarkets.

Heat oven to 210°C (200°C fanbake), with the rack just below the middle.

Cut the dried mango into thin (about 3mm) strips using a wet knife or scissors, then cut these into tiny cubes. Pour the juice over them and microwave on High (100%) power for 4 minutes, or simmer for 5 minutes. Leave to stand in the remaining juice until cool.

Measure the yoghurt and the next four ingredients into a large bowl. Add the cooled mango and its liquid, and stir everything together.

Mix the self-raising flour and sugar together in another bowl, then tip into the liquid mixture. Fold together, stopping as soon as there are no visible streaks of flour (see page 90). If the mixture looks too thick when everything is nearly mixed in, add 1–2 extra tablespoons of juice.

Divide the mixture between 12 regular muffin pans which have been well coated with non-stick spray.

Bake for 12–15 minutes, until muffins are golden brown and the centres spring back when pressed. Leave in pans for 3–5 minutes, then remove carefully and cool on a rack.

YIELD: 12 regular muffins. **SERVE:** Delicious for breakfast or brunch or with tea or coffee any time. Store cooled muffins in plastic bags.

Mango & Macadamia Muffins

Puréed, canned mango gives these muffins a delicious fruity flavour and an attractive golden colour, and keeps them wonderfully moist. Be prepared to buy more macadamia nuts than you need for the recipe – we find them so delicious that it is impossible not to sample them as we chop them!

425g can mango slices in light syrup
    or 1 cup mashed raw mango
1 cup low-fat plain or fruit-flavoured
    yoghurt
1 large egg
¼ cup canola or other oil
1 tsp vanilla

2 cups self-raising flour
1 cup sugar
½ tsp salt
about ½ cup roasted macadamia
    nuts*

* Macadamia nuts intended for snacking are
  usually lightly salted. These are fine for use in
  this recipe.

Heat oven to 210°C (200°C fanbake), with the rack just below the middle.

Drain the canned mango slices well, then transfer the mango to a medium-sized bowl and mash it with a fork. Add the yoghurt, egg, oil and vanilla and mix with the fork until everything is blended.

Measure the flour, sugar and salt into a larger bowl. Roughly chop the macadamia nuts, add these to the flour mixture, and toss well with a fork. Pour in the liquid ingredients and fold together until the flour is just moistened. Do not overmix (see page 90), as this toughens the muffins and causes them to rise in peaks as they bake, instead of being gently rounded.

Spoon the mixture into 12 muffin pans which have been well coated with non-stick spray.

Bake for 15–20 minutes until the muffins are golden brown on top and spring back when pressed in their centres. Leave to stand for 4–5 minutes in their pans, then remove carefully and cool on a rack.

YIELD: 12 regular muffins. **SERVE:** Delicious just as they are, or dust lightly with icing sugar just before serving. Freeze muffins which will not be eaten within 2–3 days.

Crunchy Lemon & Poppyseed Muffins

These delicious muffins were inspired by a number of different lemon and poppyseed loaves and cakes we have tried over the years. They are not nearly as rich as some of the 'originals' but are easy to make and still very good.

2 cups self-raising flour
1 cup sugar
½ cup poppyseeds
finely grated rind of 2 lemons

100g butter
2 large eggs
1 cup milk

juice of 2 lemons
¼ cup sugar

Heat oven to 200°C (190°C fanbake), with the rack just below the middle.

Measure the flour, sugar and poppyseeds into a large bowl. Finely grate all the coloured rind from the lemons and add to the flour mixture.

Heat the butter in a microwave dish or pot until just melted. Add the eggs and the milk and beat with a fork until everything is thoroughly combined. Tip the liquid into the dry ingredients and fold together until the flour is dampened. Do not beat till smooth (see page 90).

Spoon mixture into 12 regular muffin pans which have been lightly buttered or non-stick sprayed.

Bake for 10–15 minutes until golden brown, and until the centres spring back when pressed. While muffins cook, squeeze the lemon juice and mix with the second amount of sugar. (The sugar should not be dissolved.)

Allow the muffins to cool in their pans for 3–4 minutes, then take them out and brush the lemon and sugar mixture over their entire surfaces. Cool on a rack.

YIELD: 12 regular muffins. **SERVE:** Warm or reheated, with coffee, tea, for lunch or for dessert.

Lemon Yoghurt Muffins

These easy-to-mix, low-fat muffins owe their moist texture to non-fat yoghurt and their lovely flavour to a generous amount of lemon rind. If you don't like grating lemons by hand, peel the rind with a potato peeler, then chop it finely with the sugar in a food processor.

rind of 1 large or 2 small lemons
¾ cup sugar
¼ cup canola or other oil
1 large egg
½ tsp salt
1 cup low-fat plain yoghurt
¼ cup lemon juice
2 cups self-raising flour

Heat oven to 200°C (190°C fanbake), with the rack just below the middle.

Grate all the yellow rind from the lemon(s) into a large bowl. Add the next 6 ingredients and stir with a fork or whisk until thoroughly mixed.

Spoon the flour into a measuring cup and sprinkle it over the mixture in the bowl. Fold everything together until the flour is just mixed in, but do not mix until smooth (see page 90).

Using two large spoons, put the mixture into 12 regular or 24 mini muffin pans which have been well sprayed with non-stick spray.

Bake for 10–12 minutes or until the centres spring back when pressed and the muffins are lightly browned.

Leave to stand for 4–5 minutes, then carefully remove from pans and finish cooling on a rack. If desired, drizzle the warm muffins with a thin lemon glaze (below) while they are cooling on the rack.

LEMON GLAZE: Add 1–2 teaspoon/s of lemon juice to 2 tablespoons of icing sugar while stirring constantly, until you have an icing which is liquid enough to drizzle in a thin stream.

YIELD: 12 regular muffins. **SERVE:** Warm or reheated, glazed (above) or dusted with icing sugar. Store in a covered container when cold if not eating straight away.

Golden Orange Muffins

The wonderful golden colour of these food processor muffins will brighten the coldest day. Our muffin recipes often undergo changes as we make them, and this recipe is no exception, since we vary the liquid and additions to suit what we have on hand.

1 orange (about 200g)
1 cup sugar
1 large egg
½ cup milk or orange juice
100g butter, melted

1½ cups standard (plain) flour
1 tsp baking powder
1 tsp baking soda
½ cup sultanas
½ cup chopped walnuts (optional)

Heat oven to 200°C (190°C fanbake), with the rack just below the middle.

Cut the unpeeled orange into quarters, then each quarter into four. Put the chopped orange (skin and flesh, but no seeds) and the sugar into a food processor and process with the metal chopping blade, until the orange is very finely chopped. Add the egg, milk and melted butter and process until combined.

Sift the dry ingredients into the processor bowl, sprinkle in the sultanas and nuts, then process in short bursts, stopping as soon as the dry ingredients are dampened. Take great care not to overmix (see page 90).

Lightly butter or non-stick spray 12 regular muffin pans, then divide the mixture evenly between them.

Bake for 12–14 minutes, until golden brown and the centres spring back when pressed. Leave to stand in the pans for 3–4 minutes, then remove from the pans and cool on a rack.

VARIATION: For Orange Cream Cheese Muffins, leave out dried fruit and nuts. Half fill muffin pans with mixture, place a spoonful of cream cheese on the centre of each, then top with remaining mixture.

YIELD: 12 regular muffins. **SERVE:** Best warm. They don't need buttering.

Crunchy Lemon Muffins

These have to get the prize for being Alison's most popular muffin ever! The sugar and lemon juice brushed over the top after baking, gives them an extra-tangy flavour as well as an interesting sugary crunch.

2 cups self-raising flour
¾ cup sugar

75g butter
1 cup milk
1 large egg
grated rind of 1 large or 2 small lemons

¼ cup lemon juice
¼ cup sugar

Heat oven to 200°C (190°C fanbake), with the rack just below the middle.

Measure the flour and sugar into a bowl and toss to mix.

Melt the butter in a large bowl, then add the milk, eggs and lemon rind and beat well with a fork to combine.

Add the dry ingredients to the liquids and fold gently to combine, stopping as soon as the dry ingredients have been lightly dampened but not thoroughly mixed (see page 90).

Divide the mixture evenly between 12 regular muffin pans that have been lightly buttered or well coated with non-stick spray.

Bake for 10–12 minutes or until golden brown and until the centres spring back when pressed.

CRUNCHY LEMON GLAZE: While muffins bake, stir together the lemon juice and sugar without dissolving the sugar. Brush this over the hot muffins as soon as they are removed from the baking pans.

YIELD: 12 regular muffins. **SERVE:** With tea or coffee for afternoon tea or as a dessert served with lightly whipped cream and fresh fruit or berries.

♥ Date, Lemon & Yoghurt Muffins

Puréed dates add sweetness as well as moistness to these muffins, which have a slight lemony tang as well. A food processor makes the preparation of the liquid mixture very easy.

rind of 1 lemon
¼ cup sugar
1 cup (150g) dates, halved
½ cup boiling water
juice of 1 lemon made up to ½ cup
    with water
1 large egg
½ cup low-fat plain or apricot yoghurt
½ cup canola or other oil
½ cup crushed or finely chopped
    walnuts
½ tsp salt

1 cup self-raising flour
¾ cup wholemeal flour
2 tsp baking powder

Heat oven to 200°C (190°C fanbake), with the rack just below the middle.

With a potato peeler, peel the lemon into the food processor bowl. Add the sugar and process to finely chop the peel. Halve and add the dates (this is a double check that no stones remain in them), then add boiling water. Process to purée dates and mix the lemon rind through them. Squeeze the juice from the lemon, and make it up to ½ cup with cold water. Add it to the dates, with the egg, yoghurt and oil, and process again. Add the nuts to the food processor with the salt and process until finely ground.

Stir the flours and baking powder together in a large bowl. Tip in the mixture from the food processor, and fold it into the dry ingredients, stirring no more than is absolutely necessary. Do NOT mix until smooth (see page 90).

Spoon into 12 regular muffin pans which have been well coated with non-stick spray. If you can't fit all the mixture in the pans, leave it to stand in a cool place, without stirring it, until the first batch has cooked.

Bake for about 15 minutes, until the centres spring back when pressed, and a skewer pushed to the bottom of the largest muffin comes out clean. Leave to stand for 2–3 minutes, or until the muffins will lift out cleanly. Top with lemon glaze (page 28) or crunchy lemon glaze (page 18) if you like.

YIELD: 12–18 regular muffins. **SERVE:** Warm or cold with tea or coffee. Store in an airtight container when cool.

Lemonade & Cream Muffins

These light textured, very easy (and exceptionally good) muffins are based on a scone recipe which "did the rounds" some years ago. For a summertime treat, serve them warm, split, with jam and/or fresh strawberries and whipped cream.

2 cups self-raising flour
½ cup sugar
¼ tsp salt

½ cup fizzy lemonade
½ cup cream
1 large egg

Heat oven to 200°C (190°C fanbake), with the rack just below the middle.

Measure the flour, sugar and salt into a large bowl and toss together with a fork.

In another large bowl, mix the lemonade, cream and egg with the fork, until combined.

Tip the flour mixture into the liquid, then fold gently together until the flour is just moistened (see page 90). Spoon the mixture into 12 non-stick sprayed or buttered muffin pans.

Bake for 10–15 minutes, until muffins are a light golden colour and firm when pressed in the centre.

YIELD: 12 regular muffins. **SERVE:** Best when freshly made, especially with whipped cream and fresh strawberries.

Sticky Butterscotch & Walnut Muffins

When you want to please your family, whip up a batch of these "upside down" muffins and serve them warm, soon after you take them from the oven. It's amazing what an interesting topping can do for a perfectly plain muffin!

100g butter, melted
½ cup soft brown sugar
about ½ cup chopped walnuts

2 cups standard (plain) flour
4 tsp baking powder
½ tsp salt
¾ cup sugar

100g butter
1 large egg
1 cup milk

Heat oven to 220°C (190°C fanbake), with the rack just below the middle.

Lightly spray or butter 12 regular muffin pans. To make the topping, measure into the prepared pans about two teaspoons each of melted butter, brown sugar and chopped walnuts.

Stir the dry ingredients together in a large bowl, using a fork.

Melt the second measure of butter in a large bowl, then add the egg and milk and beat together lightly with a fork until well combined.

Tip the dry ingredients into the liquids, then fold them together until the flour is just moistened. Take care not to overmix (see page 90). Carefully spoon the mixture into the prepared pans, helping the mixture off the spoon with another spoon.

Bake 10–12 minutes, or until the centres spring back when pressed. Leave to stand for 2–3 minutes before gently rotating the muffins in their pans to make sure that the topping is attached to them and not to the pan base, then lift them out. BEWARE! The topping mixture is extremely hot! Put muffins, topping side up, on a rack

NOTE: When you bake muffins on top of a butter and sugar mixture, the muffins rise differently, and are flat on top.

YIELD: 12 regular muffins. **SERVE:** Warm (allow to cool just enough to avoid burnt lips or mouths) or reheated.

Glazed Gingerbread Muffins

These muffins may not be as dark in colour as traditional gingerbread, but the combination of fresh ginger and ginger ale gives them a definite ginger flavour. They are good as is, but are particularly delicious when glazed.

2 cups self-raising flour
½–¾ cup sugar
1 Tbsp grated fresh ginger
1 tsp mixed spice
1 tsp cinnamon

50g melted butter
1 cup ginger ale
1 large egg

OPTIONAL GLAZE:

2 tsp butter
1 tsp ground ginger
2 tsp golden syrup
2 tsp water
¼ cup icing sugar

Heat oven to 200°C (190°C fanbake), with the rack just below the middle.

Measure the flour, the desired amount of sugar, and the ginger and spices into a bowl and stir to combine evenly.

Melt the butter in another large bowl, then add the ginger ale and egg. Whisk lightly to combine.

Tip the flour mixture into the liquids, then fold gently together until the flour is just moistened (see page 90). Spoon the mixture into 12 thoroughly non-stick sprayed regular muffin pans.

Bake for 12–15 minutes until golden brown and the centres spring back when pressed.

While muffins cook, prepare the glaze by mixing together all the ingredients. Warm it to brushable consistency if necessary. As soon as the muffins are cooked, remove them from the pans and brush the glaze on their tops while they are still hot, using a pastry brush or (unused!) varnish brush.

YIELD: 12 regular muffins. **SERVE:** Best eaten the day they are made. Nice warm or reheated.

Fig & Honey Muffins

The ingredients in these muffins – tree-ripened figs, yoghurt, honey and nuts – remind us of warm days in the Greek Isles.

150g dried figs
½ cup boiling water
½ cup honey, warmed
1 large egg
¼ cup canola or other oil
2 tsp cinnamon
½ tsp salt
½ cup low-fat plain yoghurt
¼–½ cup chopped almonds

1 cup self-raising flour
¾ cup wholemeal flour
½ tsp baking soda

2 Tbsp lemon juice
2 Tbsp sugar

Heat oven to 200°C (190°C fanbake), with the rack just below the middle.

Put the figs in a microwave-proof jug or bowl, pour in the water, cover and heat on High (100%) power for 5 minutes. Set them aside to cool without draining.

Measure the honey and next six ingredients into a fairly large bowl, then beat with a fork until thoroughly mixed.

When the figs are cool enough to handle, cut off and discard their stems, then chop them finely. Put them in a one-cup measure and add enough cooking liquid to fill the cup, then stir them into the liquid mixture.

Measure the flours and the baking soda into any suitable container, stir or whisk to mix, then sprinkle this mixture over the cold liquids. Fold together until no streaks of flour are visible (see page 90), then spoon into 12 regular muffin pans which have been thoroughly non-stick sprayed.

Bake for 10–12 minutes, or until the centres spring back when lightly pressed. Leave in the pans for 2–3 minutes, while you mix the lemon juice and sugar. Carefully transfer muffins from the pans to a rack. Brush with the lemon mixture, making sure that some of the undissolved sugar is on each muffin.

YIELD: 12 regular muffins. **SERVE:** Warm or reheated, topped with a blob of yoghurt if desired. Freeze muffins that will not be eaten within 48 hours.

Spiced Date & Walnut Muffins

A little ground cardamom gives these muffins an interesting 'warm' flavour that's hard to put a finger on – but if you don't have any cardamom on hand, you can leave it out and they're still delicious.

½ cup chopped dates
½ cup boiling water
½ cup canola oil
½ cup milk or orange juice
1 large egg

1 cup standard (plain) flour
1 cup wholemeal flour
½ cup brown sugar, lightly packed
3 tsp baking powder
2 tsp cinnamon
1 tsp ground cardamom
½ tsp salt
½ cup chopped walnuts

Heat oven to 200°C (190°C fanbake), with the rack just below the middle.

Place the chopped dates in a medium-sized bowl and cover with the boiling water. Leave to stand for about 5 minutes, then add the oil, milk (or orange juice) and egg and stir to mix.

Measure the dry ingredients into a large bowl and toss them together until well mixed.

Pour the liquid mixture into the dry ingredients and fold together until just mixed (see page 90). Spoon the mixture into 12 regular muffin pans which have been coated with non-stick spray.

Bake for 12–15 minutes, or until golden brown and the centres spring back when pressed gently and a skewer comes out clean.

YIELD: 12 regular muffins. **SERVE:** Warm or reheated, great with tea or coffee.

'Pumpkin & Pecan Pie' Muffins

The flavourings in these muffins are based on those used in a classic American pumpkin pie. We thought we'd add pecans too, as they're another American favourite, but if you don't have any on hand, replace them with walnuts or just omit them completely.

1 cup (250g) cooked pumpkin, cooled
½ cup low-fat milk
¼ cup canola or other oil
1 large egg
1 tsp vanilla

1 cup standard (plain) flour
1 cup wholemeal flour
4 tsp baking powder
1 cup lightly packed brown sugar
1 tsp cinnamon
½ tsp ground ginger
½ tsp ground cloves
½ tsp salt
½ cup chopped pecans

Heat oven to 210°C (200°C fanbake), with the rack just below the middle.

To cook the pumpkin, wrap it (skin-on) in baking paper and microwave on High (100%) power for about 4 minutes, or until soft when squeezed. Leave to stand until cool, then peel off the skin.

Put the cooled pumpkin, milk, oil, egg and vanilla in a food processor and process until smooth (or mash well with a fork or potato masher).

Measure the flours into a large bowl. Add the baking powder, sugar, spices and salt and stir with a whisk or fork to combine.

Pour the liquids into the dry ingredients, sprinkle in the chopped pecans, and gently fold together. Mix just enough to moisten the flour (see page 90). Spoon the mixture into 12 regular or 24 mini muffin pans that have been thoroughly non-stick sprayed.

Bake for 12–15 minutes until tops begin to brown and the centres spring back when pressed (test to see if a skewer poked into the middle of a muffin comes out clean if you are unsure).

Cool in their pans for 2–3 minutes before tipping out and cooling on a rack.

YIELD: 12 regular or 24 mini muffins. **SERVE:** Warm or cold, freezing any that will not be eaten within 24 hours of baking.

Maple Walnut Muffins

These are possibly some of our best ever muffins! This is especially pleasing considering they are low-fat and relatively high in fibre.

1½ cups wholemeal flour
1 cup All-Bran type cereal*
1 cup walnut pieces
½ cup brown sugar
½ tsp baking soda
1 tsp baking powder
¾ tsp salt

½ cup maple syrup**
½ cup canola or other oil
½ cup natural low-fat yoghurt
1 large egg or 2 egg whites

* We use an extruded mixed bran cereal as our first choice, and extruded wheat bran (All-Bran) when this is not available.
**Use "Real" or maple "flavoured" syrup.

Heat oven to 200°C (190°C fanbake), with the rack just below the middle.

Measure the flour, bran cereal, walnut pieces and sugar into a large bowl. Sift in the baking soda, baking powder and salt, then stir until evenly combined.

Combine the syrup, oil, yoghurt and egg (or egg whites) in another bowl and whisk to combine. Pour the liquid mixture into the dry ingredients and fold everything together. Take care not to overmix (see page 90).

Spoon the mixture into 12 non-stick sprayed or oiled muffin pans.

Bake for 12 minutes or until firm when pressed in the centre.

NOTE: The maple syrup may cause these muffins to brown quickly and darken too much if they are cooked for too long or at too high a temperature. Reduce the heat during baking if necessary.

YIELD: 12 generous regular muffins. **SERVE:** Any time, with tea or coffee.

♥ Blueberry Bran Muffins

Here is our version of a classic American favourite. Every time I eat one I can understand their popularity! Keep a packet of blueberries in your freezer, so you can make a batch of these at short notice.

1 cup baking bran (wheat bran)
¼ cup wheatgerm or extra bran
½ cup canola or other oil
1 cup plain or fruity yoghurt
1 large egg

¾ cup wholemeal flour
¾ cup high grade (bread) flour
1 tsp cinnamon
1 tsp baking powder
¾ tsp salt
½ tsp baking soda
1 cup brown sugar
1–1½ cups (150–180g) frozen
    blueberries

Heat oven to 200°C (190°C fanbake), with the rack just below the middle.

Measure the first five ingredients into a large bowl, mix to blend everything with a fork, then leave to stand. (If you don't have wheatgerm in the house, replace it with extra bran.)

Measure the remaining dry ingredients into a medium-sized bowl, and stir well with a fork to mix thoroughly. Do not thaw the blueberries, but separate any clumps of berries. (We use half a 350g packet and find that this is a very good amount for this recipe, although you can use less.)

Tip the flour mixture into the liquid mixture, then fold everything together until the dry ingredients are moistened without overmixing (see page 90).

Spoon the mixture into 12–15 regular or about 30 mini muffin pans which have been thoroughly non-stick sprayed.

Bake for about 15 minutes (longer than most other muffins, because of the frozen berries in the mixture), until centres spring back when pressed.

YIELD: 12–15 regular or 30 mini muffins. **SERVE:** Warm or reheated, without any spread, at any time of the day.

♥ Bulk Bran Muffins

This recipe makes about three dozen regular muffins. You can refrigerate the uncooked mixture for up to two weeks, cooking them as required. As the muffins can be microwaved, hungry children can cook their own muffins from the refrigerated mixture.

½ cup treacle
2 cups rolled oats
1 cup baking bran (wheat bran)
1 cup boiling water
1 cup brown sugar
2 Tbsp wine vinegar
1 tsp salt
2 large eggs
2 cups milk
2 cups standard (plain) flour
1 cup oat bran
1½ tsp baking soda

Heat oven to 220°C (210°C fanbake), with the rack just below the middle.

Measure the treacle, rolled oats and baking bran into a large bowl. Pour over boiling water and stir until treacle and oats are mixed. Leave to cool for 5 minutes, then add the brown sugar, vinegar, salt and eggs. Beat with a fork to combine eggs.

Add the milk and then the flour, oat bran and baking soda, previously forked together. Stir only enough to combine (see page 90).

Spray muffin pans with non-stick spray. Put about ¼ cup of mixture into each muffin cup.

Bake for about 10 minutes, until muffins spring back when pressed.

OR Microwave in paper cases in microwave muffin moulds, for about 2 minutes on High (100%) power for 5 muffins. Microwave ovens vary – experiment with the first few batches you make until you know the exact time taken by your microwave oven. Always leave to stand for a few minutes before removing muffins from pans.

YIELD: 36 regular or 72 mini muffins. **SERVE:** Warm for breakfast, brunch, with coffee, in lunches or after school. Serve microwaved muffins within 30 minutes of cooking.

Eggless Bran Muffins

Warm from the oven, these plain, old-fashioned muffins make a very low-fat weekend breakfast or lunch. They have a lovely golden syrup flavour but each muffin contains nearly three tablespoons of bran, so is really high in fibre - and they contain no egg, butter or oil!

¾ cup golden syrup
½ cup boiling water
1 cup low-fat milk

2 cups baking bran (wheat bran)
1 cup plain flour
1 tsp baking powder
1 tsp baking soda
1 tsp salt

Heat oven to 210°C (200°C fanbake), with the rack just below the middle.

Measure the golden syrup into a large bowl (pour hot water over a ¼ cup measure, before dipping it into the tin of syrup). Add the boiling water and stir until syrup is dissolved. Add the milk and stir again.

Measure the remaining ingredients into another bowl (measure the baking soda into the palm of your hand and squash it with the back of the measuring spoon to ensure there are no lumps, before adding it to the bowl). Mix the dry ingredients together thoroughly.

Thoroughly non-stick spray 12 regular muffin pans. Tip all the dry ingredients into the cool milk mixture. Fold the dry ingredients into the wet mixture until all the bran and flour is dampened. Do not overmix or stir until smooth. (Expect a larger, more liquid mixture than normal.) Using two spoons, divide the mixture equally between the muffin pans.

Bake for 12–15 minutes, until muffins are an attractive brown colour and they spring back when pressed. Because the mixture is fairly wet, the muffin tops may be flatter than usual. Leave muffins to stand in the pans for 3–4 minutes, then carefully transfer to a cooling rack. Put in plastic bags when cold.

VARIATION: Add ½ cup of small dark raisins or sultanas to the syrup mixture. And/or: Add ¼–½ cup chopped walnuts to the bran and flour mixture.

YIELD: 12 regular muffins. **SERVE:** Warm (or reheated). Cottage cheese makes a good low-fat topping. Freeze any muffins you do not expect to eat within two days.

Nearly No-Fat Banana Bran Muffins

Alison often made these during cooking shows to prove that muffins which contain no butter or oil as well as a lot of bran can be moist and taste absolutely delicious. Try them yourself and see!

2 cups baking bran (wheat bran)
½ cup sultanas
½ cup chopped nuts
½ cup flour
1 tsp baking powder
1 tsp baking soda
1 tsp cinnamon

½ cup golden syrup
1 cup milk
1 large egg or 2 egg whites*
2 large bananas, mashed

* For diets which exclude egg yolks, use two large egg whites instead.

Heat oven to 200°C (190°C fanbake), with the rack just below the middle.

Measure the bran into a large bowl, then add the sultanas and nuts. Measure the flour, baking powder, baking soda and cinnamon into a sieve over the bowl, shake them onto the bran, and stir to mix evenly.

Warm the tin of golden syrup in a bowl of hot water until it is runny, then measure what you need into another large bowl (use a hot, wet measuring cup for ease). Add the milk and egg and beat with a fork until well mixed. Mash the bananas with a fork, on a board or plate, and stir into the liquid.

Tip the dry ingredients into the liquid mixture and fold together just until bran is evenly dampened. Do not overmix (see page 90).

Divide the mixture evenly into 18 regular (or 36 mini) thoroughly non-stick sprayed muffin pans using two spoons.

Bake for about 7 minutes for mini muffins and 10 minutes for regular muffins, or until muffins spring back when pressed in the middle. Watch carefully during cooking, since muffins containing a lot of golden syrup burn easily. Leave for 2–3 minutes before twisting and removing from pans.

YIELD: 18 regular or 36 mini muffins. **SERVE:** Eat warm, freezing extras. Spread large muffins with low-fat cottage cheese; serve mini muffins plain.

Basic Bran Muffins

These bran muffins are very easy and quick to make. Because they have no added butter or oil they stick easily, so take care to prepare the muffin pans carefully. For a real treat, spread these muffins with creamy (but low-fat) cottage cheese or quark, and top with red currant or crabapple jelly!

2 cups baking bran (wheat bran)
½ cup standard (plain) flour
1 tsp baking powder
1 tsp baking soda
½ cup sultanas (optional)
¼ cup chopped walnuts (optional)

½ cup golden syrup or treacle
1 large egg
1 cup milk

Heat oven to 200°C (190°C fanbake), with the rack just below the middle.

Put the bran into a large mixing bowl, then sieve onto the bran the next three dry ingredients. Add the sultanas and/or walnuts if you are using them, then mix everything together lightly using your fingers.

Warm the golden syrup or treacle in a saucepan or microwave bowl until runny. Remove from the heat, then add the egg and milk and mix well. Pour the liquids onto the dry ingredients and fold together only until the dry ingredients are barely dampened (see page 90).

Divide the mixture evenly between 12 regular muffin pans that have been well coated with non-stick spray.

Bake for about 10–15 minutes or until firm in the middle when pressed lightly.

YIELD: 12 regular or 24 mini muffins. **SERVE:** For brunch, with tea or coffee or at any time of the day. Excellent in packed lunches. Eat within 48 hours.

Banana Bran Muffins

These muffins are delicious! When they are freshly made you can serve them just as they are, without butter or any other toppings, because they taste so good.

¾ cup standard (plain) flour
¾ cup wholemeal flour
¾ cup brown sugar
½ cup baking bran (wheat bran)
2 tsp baking powder
2 tsp cinnamon
½ cup chopped walnuts (optional)
½ cup sultanas (optional)

50g butter
1 egg
1½ cups mashed banana
1 tsp vanilla
milk, as required

Heat oven to 200°C (190°C fanbake), with the rack just below the middle.

Measure all the dry ingredients into a large bowl. Add the chopped walnuts and sultanas. Mix thoroughly with your fingers to combine.

Melt the butter in another large bowl, then stir in the egg and mix well with a fork. Add the mashed banana and vanilla and mix again.

Stir the dry ingredients into the liquid and, without overmixing, fold everything together (see page 90). (If you use barely ripe bananas you may need to add milk until you have a mixture of normal muffin consistency.)

Divide the mixture evenly between 12 regular muffin pans that have been well coated with non-stick spray.

Bake for 10–15 minutes or until the centres spring back when lightly pressed.

SIZE: 12 regular or 24 mini muffins. **SERVE:** Suitable for breakfast, brunch, or lunch, or with coffee, in packed lunches, and as an after school snack.

Oaty Refrigerator Low-Fat Muffins

Treacle gives these muffins a rich flavour, as well as enough colour to enable them to be microwaved. You can refrigerate the uncooked mixture for a week if you prefer to enjoy just a few freshly baked muffins each day.

½ cup treacle
1½ cups baking bran (wheat bran)
1 cup boiling water

1 cup brown sugar
2 Tbsp wine vinegar
1 tsp salt
2 large eggs
2 cups milk

2 cups standard (plain) flour
1 cup rolled oats
1 cup oat bran
½ cup wheatgerm
1½ tsp baking soda

Measure the treacle and bran into a large bowl. Pour over the boiling water and mix until combined. Cool for about 5 minutes. Add the sugar, wine vinegar, salt, eggs and milk and beat well with a fork.

In another bowl toss together the next five ingredients with a fork, mixing them well. Tip in the liquid ingredients and fold everything together, stirring only enough to combine (see page 90). Cover and refrigerate overnight or for up to a week before baking.

Without further mixing, spoon mixture, as required, into lightly buttered or well sprayed muffin pans.

Bake at 200°C for 10–15 minutes or until the centres spring back when pressed. Refrigerate unused mixture promptly. To microwave 4 muffins, spoon ¼ cup of mixture into Teflon lined glass ramekins, cover with cling film pierced with several holes, and cook on High (100%) power for 2 minutes or until firm.

NOTE: Microwaved muffins have their limitations, but they are convenient when only a few muffins are required.

YIELD: About 30 regular muffins. **SERVE:** Warm, soon after cooking, for breakfast, morning coffee or brunch.

Sultana & Apple Bran Muffins

Don't worry about the appearance of these fruity, moist and delicious muffins – they are meant to have flat tops! Enjoy their flavour and texture, eating them just as they are, without any toppings, for breakfast, in packed lunches, as an after school snack, or with a cup of coffee.

1 cup sultanas
1 large egg
½ cup low-fat plain yoghurt
½ cup canola or other oil
2 tsp cinnamon
2 tsp mixed spice
½ tsp salt
1 large (tangy) apple

¾ cup brown sugar
1 cup baking bran (wheat bran)
1 cup standard (plain) flour
1 tsp baking soda
½ cup walnuts, roughly chopped
  (optional)

Heat oven to 200°C (190°C fanbake), with the rack just below the middle.

Measure the sultanas into a large bowl, cover with boiling water, and leave to stand.

Put the egg and the next five ingredients into a medium-sized bowl, beat with a fork to mix, then grate the unpeeled apple and stir it through the liquid mixture, working quickly to stop the apple browning.

Drain the sultanas, pat dry with a paper towel, then stir them into the apple mixture. Dry the large bowl and measure in the sugar, bran, flour and baking soda. Add the walnuts, if using. Mix all the dry ingredients together, making sure that there are no lumps of sugar or soda.

Tip the liquid mixture into the dry ingredients, then fold everything together, mixing just enough to dampen the dry ingredients (see page 90).

Using two large spoons, divide the mixture between 12 regular-sized muffin pans which have been well sprayed with non-stick spray.

Bake for 12–15 minutes, or until the tops spring back when pressed in the middle. Leave in the pans for 3–5 minutes, then lift out and cool on a rack.

YIELD: 12 regular muffins. **SERVE:** Warm or reheated for breakfast or lunch. Freeze or eat within two days.

Kumara, Bacon & Onion Muffins

There is something memorable about these muffins! They have a mild but distinctive flavour and texture, and are a very popular addition to luncheon buffets, especially when overseas visitors are present.

2 Tbsp canola or other oil
2 rashers (100g) lean bacon, chopped
1 small onion

2 cups self-raising flour
1 cup grated tasty cheese
1 tsp mild curry powder
½ tsp salt

1 cup milk
1 large egg
1 cup (200g) roughly mashed cooked kumara*

Heat oven to 200°C (190°C fanbake), with the rack just below the middle.

Heat the oil in a medium-sized frypan. Cook the chopped bacon and finely chopped onion in it, stirring occasionally, until bacon begins to brown.

Meanwhile, measure the flour, grated cheese, curry powder and salt into a large bowl. Toss well with a fork to mix.

In another bowl mix the milk and egg with the fork until blended, then stir in the roughly mashed kumara, and mix again, leaving some chunky pieces.

Tip the cooked bacon and onion, then the flour, into the kumara mixture. Gently fold everything together until the flour is just moistened. Do not overmix (see page 90).

Spoon the mixture into 12 lightly buttered or non-stick sprayed regular-sized muffin pans or 24 mini muffin pans.

Bake for 12–15 minutes, or until golden brown on top and firm when pressed in the centre.

YIELD: 12 regular or 24 mini muffins. **SERVE:** See introduction. Good flavour when hot, warm or cold. Buttering is not necessary.

* Use Golden Kumara for a definite gold colour. For easy preparation, scrub about 300g of kumara, cut off any hairy protrusions, then microwave for 4-5 minutes, until the flesh in the thickest part "gives" when gently squeezed. When cool, peel off skin and mash roughly.

Avocado & Bacon Muffins

Everybody seems to like the combination of avocados, cheese, bacon and spring onions – these are always popular. Serve them with fruit and a drink as a complete lunch.

2 cups standard (plain) flour
4 tsp baking powder
½ tsp salt
1 Tbsp sugar
pinch of cayenne pepper
1 cup (100g) grated tasty cheese
4 spring onions, chopped
3 rashers bacon

75g butter
1 large egg
1 cup milk
1 avocado
about 1 Tbsp lemon juice

Heat oven to 200°C (190°C fanbake), with the rack just below the middle.

Sieve the first four (dry) ingredients into a large bowl. Add the cayenne pepper, grated cheese and chopped spring onion, and stir to combine.

Chop the bacon finely and cook in a frypan or under the grill until crisp. Keep the bacon drippings.

Melt the butter in another large bowl, add the egg, milk and bacon drippings, and beat to combine. Halve the avocado, then scoop out the flesh with a dessert or tablespoon and cut into 7mm cubes. Sprinkle with lemon juice to stop cubes from browning. Add to the liquid mixture.

Add the bacon and the flour mixture to the liquid ingredients and fold together. Stir only to dampen the flour (see page 90).

Spray 12 regular or 24 mini muffin pans with non-stick spray, then place spoonfuls of mixture into them.

Bake for about 10 minutes, or until the muffins spring back when pressed lightly in the centre.

YIELD: 12 regular or 24 mini muffins. **SERVE:** Always warm, as finger food with drinks, or as the main part of lunch.

Herbed Chicken & Cranberry Muffins

▶

Make these unusual, savoury muffins with the last of a festive chicken (or turkey) or a smoked chicken breast. Alternatively, for something a little different, leave out the chicken and make mini muffins to serve with roast poultry, instead of stuffing and cranberry sauce.

2 cups standard (plain) flour
3 tsp baking powder
½ tsp salt
¼ cup chopped fresh herbs (half parsley, half thyme or marjoram etc.)
black pepper
1 cup (150g) chopped cooked chicken

75g butter
½ medium onion, diced
225g jar whole cranberry sauce

1 large egg
½ cup milk

Heat oven to 200°C (190°C fanbake), with the rack just below the middle.

Sift the flour, baking powder and salt into a large bowl. Add the chopped fresh herbs, freshly ground black pepper to taste and the chopped cooked (plain or smoked) chicken. Toss together until evenly mixed.

Melt the butter in a medium-sized frypan, add the diced onion and cook for 2–3 minutes until the onion is soft. Reduce the heat and spoon in the cranberry sauce. Heat, stirring gently until the sauce has just melted.

Whisk the egg and milk together in another large bowl, stir in the warm cranberry mixture, then sprinkle in the dry ingredients.

Gently fold everything together until the flour is just dampened. Take care not to overmix (see page 90). Spoon the mixture into 10 regular or 24 mini muffin pans which have been non-stick sprayed or lightly buttered.

Bake for 12 minutes or until lightly browned and firm when pressed in the centre.

VARIATION: Add ¼–½ cup of dried cranberries.

YIELD: 10 regular or 24 mini muffins. **SERVE:** Warm, with a salad, for lunch. If made without the chicken, serve warm with roast poultry. Good at a buffet meal.

Hawaiian Ham Muffins

Shut your eyes and be transported to a tropical island with white sands, waving palms, soft guitar music and undulating hips or, more prosaically, remember that "Hawaiian" is the name used for a combination of ham, pineapple and cheese!

2 cups standard (plain) flour
4 tsp baking powder
½ tsp salt
about 100g ham or ham pieces, diced
1½ cups grated tasty cheese
2 spring onions, chopped

300g can crushed pineapple
about ¾ cup coconut cream or milk
1 large egg

Heat oven to 210°C (200°C fanbake), with the rack just below the middle.

Measure the dry ingredients into a large bowl. Add the diced ham and grated cheese. Chop and add the green leaves as well as the white part of the spring onions. Using a fork, toss everything together until evenly combined.

Drain the pineapple, reserving the juice. Make the juice up to 1 cup with coconut cream or milk. Put the crushed pineapple, liquid and egg in another large bowl and mix until well combined, again using the fork.

Sprinkle the flour mixture over the liquids and fold together until the flour is just moistened, taking care to avoid overmixing (see page 90).

Spoon the mixture into 12 regular or 24 mini muffin pans which have been sprayed or lightly buttered. Top with a little extra grated cheese if you like.

Bake for 12–15 minutes, or until tops and sides are brown, and the centres spring back when lightly pressed. Leave to stand in their pans for 3–4 minutes before removing and cooling on a rack.

YIELD: 12 regular or 24 mini muffins. **SERVE:** As party finger food; with a hot or cold drink at any time of day; or as the main part of a weekend brunch or lunch, with or without a salad.

Chilli Cheese Mini Muffins

These little muffins, made with strongly-flavoured cheddar cheese, are quickly mixed and baked, and fill the house with an irresistible aroma. For best flavour and texture serve them warm (but not hot) from the oven, or reheated, up to a day later.

2 cups (200g) grated tasty cheese
1½ cups self-raising flour
1 tsp garlic salt

2 Tbsp Thai sweet chilli sauce
1 cup milk
1 large egg

Heat oven to 210°C (200°C fanbake), with the rack just below the middle.

Measure the grated cheese, flour and garlic salt into a large bowl and toss gently to combine well.

Measure the Thai sweet chilli sauce, milk and egg into a smaller bowl and beat with a fork until thoroughly combined. Pour the liquid mixture into the dry ingredients all at once, then fold everything together, mixing no more than necessary to dampen the flour (see page 90).

Thoroughly non-stick spray 24 mini muffin pans. Using two dessertspoons, divide the mixture evenly between the pans.

Bake for about 12 minutes, until the centres spring back when pressed and the muffins are golden brown. For easy removal from pans, leave muffins to stand 2–4 minutes before lifting out. (Some cheese may stick to the edges of the muffin tin. Remove it carefully.)

VARIATION: Add 2 tablespoons of chopped fresh herbs to the dry ingredients.

YIELD: 24 mini muffins. **SERVE:** Exactly as they come from the oven, OR slash deeply from the top and insert a piece of cold-smoked salmon, salami, ham, cheese, and/or a slice of a small tomato or a piece of roasted pepper, with a fresh herb leaf.

Champion Cheese Muffins

Everybody loves these muffins and they are easy enough to make often. They look even more inviting if you add a topping of grated cheese and a sprinkling of paprika or a pinch of chilli powder.

If you make these muffins regularly, buy pre-grated tasty cheese to use in them. This will save you precious minutes as well as the skin on your knuckles.

2 cups (200g) grated tasty cheese
1½ cups self-raising flour
½ tsp salt
1 Tbsp sugar
pinch of cayenne pepper

1 large egg
1 cup milk

Heat oven to 210°C (200°C fanbake), with the rack just below the middle.

Measure the grated cheese, self-raising flour, salt, sugar and cayenne pepper into a large bowl. Mix lightly with your fingertips to combine.

In another large bowl beat the egg and milk until evenly combined. Sprinkle the flour and cheese mixture over the liquids, then fold the two mixtures together, taking care not to overmix (see page 90).

Spoon mixture into 12 regular muffin pans, which have been sprayed with non-stick spray.

OPTIONAL TOPPING: Sprinkle with a little extra cheese and paprika or chilli powder before baking.

Bake for about 12 minutes, until muffins spring back when pressed in the middle and are golden brown. Leave to stand in the pans for 3–4 minutes before removing to a rack.

YIELD: 12 regular or 24 mini muffins. **SERVE:** Mini muffins for cocktail snacks and afternoon tea; regular muffins for general use or if making to freeze.

Easy Cheesy Muffins

Top

Some years ago, during a bakers' strike, an easy bread made from self-raising flour and beer "did the rounds". Starting with the same basic ingredients, you can make wonderful cheesy muffins!

2 cups self-raising flour
2 cups (200g) grated tasty cheese

1 large egg
1 cup lager or beer
about 2 Tbsp chutney (optional)

Heat the oven to 220°C (210°C fanbake), with the rack just below the middle.

Toss the flour and grated cheese together in a large bowl.

Break the egg into another large bowl and beat with a fork enough to thoroughly mix the white and yolk. Add the lager or beer (which can be flat or bubbly) and stir to mix briefly, then sprinkle in the flour and cheese mixture.

Fold together until most of the flour is dampened, but do not overmix (see details of mixing and baking on page 90). If you like the idea, drizzle your favourite chutney over the surface, and fold it in lightly so that it stays in streaks.

Spoon the mixture into 12 buttered or sprayed regular muffin pans.

Bake for 10–15 minutes, until the muffins are nicely browned and the centres spring back when pressed.

YIELD: 12 generous regular muffins or 24 mini muffins. **SERVE:** Warm or cold, very popular for lunch. Warm mini muffins make excellent party snacks.

Zucchini & Parmesan Muffins

Bottom

These muffins, flecked with pale green, are light, pretty and fresh tasting, perfect for serving on a summer's day. You'll find them especially appealing if your family has seen enough zucchini from the garden on their dinner plates!

2 cups standard (plain) flour
4 tsp baking powder
½ tsp salt
black pepper to taste
1 cup grated tasty cheese
¼ cup grated Parmesan

¾ cup milk
2 large eggs
3 zucchini, grated (250g altogether)

Heat oven to 210°C (200°C fanbake), with the rack just below the middle.

Sift or fork together the flour, baking powder and salt in a large bowl. Grind in black pepper to taste, then add the grated cheeses and stir to combine.

Break the eggs into another large bowl, add the milk and whisk together with a fork, then add the grated unpeeled zucchini.

Tip the dry ingredients into the liquid mixture, then carefully fold everything together, taking care not to overmix (see page 90). As soon as all the flour is moistened, spoon the mixture into 12 lightly buttered or non-stick sprayed regular muffin pans or 24 mini muffin pans.

Bake for 12–15 minutes, or until the tops are golden and the muffins spring back when pressed in the centre.

NOTE: If you like freshly ground pepper, use plenty in these muffins!

YIELD: 12 regular or 24 mini muffins. **SERVE:** Nice cold or warm, enjoy as they are or topped with sliced tomato and herbs. Good for picnic lunches.

Broccoli & Blue Cheese Muffins

Neither the blue cheese nor broccoli flavours of these muffins are too strong. In fact, the very pleasant savoury taste should appeal even to those who are not convinced about the merits of either.

200g broccoli (1 small-medium head)
1½ cups low-fat plain yoghurt
¼ cup canola oil
1 large egg
50g creamy blue cheese

2 cups self-raising flour
½ tsp salt

¼ cup milk, if required

Heat oven to 200°C (190°C fanbake), with the rack just below the middle.

To cook the broccoli separate it into florets and place in a microwave-safe container with 1 tablespoon of water, cover, and microwave for about 3 minutes or until very tender. Alternatively, boil or steam until tender, then drain well.

Place the yoghurt, oil and egg in a food processor and mix well. Add the broccoli, and roughly crumble in the blue cheese. Process in short bursts until there are no large pieces of broccoli left. Try not to purée the broccoli; just chop it finely.

Measure the flour and salt into a large bowl and toss together with a fork. Pour in the liquid mixture and begin to fold together. If you think the mixture looks too dry, add the extra milk and fold JUST enough to combine (see page 90).

Spray 12 regular or 24 mini muffin trays with non-stick spray. Divide the mixture evenly between the pans.

Bake for 12–15 minutes or until golden brown and centres spring back when pressed. Remove muffins from the oven and cool in their pans for 2–3 minutes before tipping out. Store cooled muffins in a plastic bag to prevent them drying out.

YIELD: 12 regular or 24 mini muffins. **SERVE:** Warm or reheated with soup or salad for a weekend lunch, or include in packed lunches.

Spinach & Feta Muffins

It's hard to know what makes the combination of spinach and feta cheese work so well, but it does! The green flecks from the spinach make these muffins look really good too.

½ cup (100–125g) cooked spinach, chopped*
1 cup (250g) lite cottage cheese
1 cup milk
¼ cup canola oil
1 large egg
50-75g feta cheese, cubed or crumbled

1 cup wholemeal flour
1 cup plain flour
4 tsp baking powder
½–1 tsp salt

* For convenience try using ½ a 250g block of frozen spinach.

Heat oven to 210°C (200°C fanbake), with the rack just below the middle.

Lightly squeeze the cooked spinach, reserving the liquid. Make the spinach liquid up to 1 cup with milk, then place the spinach, milk and spinach liquid, cottage cheese, oil and egg in a large bowl and mix well. Add the cubed or crumbled cheese and mix lightly.

Measure the flours, baking powder and salt together into another bowl and toss together with a whisk or fork.

Tip the flour mixture into the liquids, then fold gently together until the flour is just moistened. The mixture does not need to be smooth (see page 90).

Spoon the mixture into 12 non-stick sprayed regular muffin pans.

Bake for 15 minutes or until golden brown and a skewer poked into the centre of a muffin comes out clean.

Remove muffins from the oven and leave to cool in their pans for 2-3 minutes before tipping out and cooling on a rack.

NOTE: These muffins do seem to stick to their pans when first removed from the oven, but standing for a few minutes really does help removal.

YIELD: 12 regular muffins. **SERVE:** Delicious warm, or store cooled muffins in sealed bags to prevent drying out.

♥ Olive, Pesto & Feta Muffins

When you think about savoury muffins, cheese muffins tend to be the first to spring to mind. However, standard cheddar-cheesy muffins tend to be relatively high in fat so we concocted these – they still taste great and use a relatively small amount of lower-fat feta cheese instead.

2 cups self-raising flour
½ tsp salt
50–100g feta cheese, crumbled or cubed
¼ cup chopped black olives
1 cup low-fat plain yoghurt
¼ cup olive oil
1 large egg
2 Tbsp pesto

Heat oven to 210°C (200°C fanbake), with the rack just below the middle.

Measure the flour and salt into a large bowl. Add the crumbled or cubed feta and chopped olives, then stir until well mixed.

In another bowl, mix together the yoghurt, oil, egg and pesto.

Pour the liquid mixture into the dry ingredients, then stir gently until just mixed (stop as soon as all the flour has been moistened).

Spoon the mixture into 12 regular muffin pans which have been well sprayed with non-stick spray.

Bake for 12–15 minutes, or until the tops are golden brown and the centres are firm when pressed.

Leave to stand for a couple of minutes, then remove from the pans and cool on a wire rack.

YIELD: 12 regular muffins. **SERVE:** Enjoy them warm, or bag and freeze any muffins you do not intend to eat within 24 hours.

Asparagus Luncheon Muffins

Both canned and fresh asparagus gives muffins a distinctive flavour. These are unusual and interesting, as well as popular.

2 cups self-raising flour
1 cup (100g) grated tasty cheese
2 spring onions, chopped
¼ tsp cayenne pepper
½ tsp salt

340g can asparagus
¼ cup sour cream
2 large eggs

Heat oven to 200°C (190°C fanbake), with the rack just below the middle.

Measure the flour, cheese, spring onions, cayenne pepper and salt into a fairly large bowl. Toss together with a fork to combine.

Drain the asparagus (retaining the liquid) and chop stalks into 5mm pieces.

Make the asparagus liquid up to ¾ cup with water if necessary, and mix this with the sour cream and eggs in another large bowl.

Sprinkle the chopped asparagus and flour mixture into the liquid ingredients. Without overmixing (see page 90), fold everything together, taking care not to mash the asparagus pieces.

Spray 12 regular muffin pans with non-stick spray. Put about ¼ cup of mixture into each muffin cup.

Bake for 12–15 minutes, until muffins spring back when pressed.

VARIATION: Cut 200g of fresh asparagus into 5mm slices, and cook in about ½ cup of lightly salted water until just tender. Use cooking liquid as above.

YIELD: 12 regular or 24 mini muffins. **SERVE:** Warm as finger food for parties, or as the main part of lunch.

Golden Cornmeal Muffins

These muffins make a good summer lunch, especially when served outdoors with salads. The yellow cornmeal gives them a slight grittiness which sounds odd but is actually very nice. (Do not use very fine, flour-like cornmeal for this recipe.)

1 cup standard or wholemeal flour
½ cup yellow cornmeal
3 tsp baking powder
1 cup (100g) grated tasty cheese
¼ cup sugar
¼ tsp salt

50g butter
1 large egg
½ cup creamed corn
½ cup plain yoghurt or milk

Heat oven to 210°C (200°C fanbake), with the rack just below the middle.

Measure the flour, cornmeal, baking powder, cheese, sugar and salt into a large mixing bowl. Toss well with a fork.

Melt the butter in another large bowl. Add the egg, creamed corn and yoghurt or milk (add yoghurt in preference to milk – it makes muffins more tender), then mix with a fork.

Fold the liquid mixture into the dry ingredients, taking great care not to overmix (see page 90).

Thoroughly non-stick spray 12 regular muffin pans, then put about ¼ cup of mixture in each muffin cup.

Bake for 10–15 minutes, until quite crusty and nicely browned. Leave to stand in the pans for about 3 minutes before removing and cooling on a wire rack.

YIELD: 12 regular or 24 mini muffins. **SERVE:** Warm as finger food at parties, or serve for lunch, as part of a buffet, or as picnic food.

Pizza Muffins

If your family and friends like pizza (and who doesn't), we're sure you will find that these muffins "go down a treat" for lunch or with coffee.

2 cups grated tasty cheese
2 cups standard (plain) flour
3 tsp baking powder
1 Tbsp sugar
1 spring onion, chopped (white and
    green parts)
50g salami, finely chopped
½ tsp dried oregano, crumbled

1 Tbsp tomato paste
3 Tbsp water
1 cup milk
1 large egg

OPTIONAL TOPPING:

½ medium tomato, deseeded and
    finely chopped
about ½ cup grated cheese
2–3 slices salami, chopped

Heat oven to 220°C (210°C fanbake), with the rack just below the middle.

Measure the grated cheese, flour, baking powder and sugar into a large bowl. Add the spring onion, salami and oregano, then stir lightly to combine.

Mix the tomato paste and water until smooth in another large bowl. Add the milk and egg, and beat with the fork until well combined.

Pour the flour mixture into this liquid and fold together until the flour is moistened. Take care not to overmix (see page 90)!

Spoon the mixture into 12 regular or 24 mini muffin pans that have been thoroughly non-stick sprayed.

If you have the time and inclination, place a few pieces of tomato, a few shreds of grated cheese and a couple of pieces of salami on each muffin.

Bake for 12 minutes, or until lightly browned on top and firm when pressed in the middle.

YIELD: 12 regular or 24 mini muffins. **SERVE:** Irresistible hot from the oven, but the flavour is even better when cold.

friands

Raspberry & Vanilla Friands

Friands seem to be rapidly gaining in popularity. I don't know whether they will ever completely replace muffins in our psyche or kitchens, but they are delicious and make a good occasional treat.

100g butter, melted
1 cup ground almonds
1 cup sugar
1 tsp vanilla
¼ cup milk
3 eggs
¼ tsp salt
½ cup self-raising flour
12–24 fresh or frozen raspberries*

* Raspberries can be replaced with other berries or fruit – blueberries and halved strawberries work well.

Heat oven to 180°C (190°C fanbake), with the rack just below the middle.

Melt the butter in a medium-sized bowl. Add the almonds, sugar, vanilla, and milk to the butter and stir until well combined.

Separate the eggs, stirring the yolks into the almond mixture, and putting the whites into another large clean bowl (any traces of fat will prevent the whites fluffing up). Add the salt, then beat the whites with an egg beater until they form stiff peaks.

Sprinkle the flour over the whites, then pour or spoon in the almond mixture and gently fold everything together just enough to combine.

Thoroughly non-stick spray 12 friand or muffin pans (it pays to do this carefully because they do seem to have a tendency to stick) and divide the mixture between them. Place one or two raspberries on the top of each, then place in the oven and bake for 12–15 minutes until golden brown and the centres spring back when pressed.

Remove from the oven and leave to cool for 3–5 minutes to make them easier to remove, before turning them out of the pans to cool on a rack.

YIELD: 12 friands. **SERVE:** Dust with icing sugar and serve warm or cold at any time; particularly good with tea or coffee.

Chocolate & Hazelnut Friands

Friands are traditionally made using ground almonds, but hazelnuts work really well too, especially when paired with chocolate. Try them warm from the oven so the chocolate centre is still soft.

1 cup (140g) toasted hazelnuts*
100g dark chocolate, melted
25g butter
¾ cup sugar
1 tsp vanilla
¼ cup milk
3 eggs
¼ tsp salt
½ cup self-raising flour
6–12 squares (30-60g) chocolate (optional)

* To toast the hazelnuts, tip them into a sponge roll tin and place them in the oven as it heats. Keep a close watch on them, as nuts can burn quickly. Remove them from the oven as soon as they have darkened visibly.

Heat oven to 180°C (170°C fanbake), with the rack just below the middle.

Place the hazelnuts in a food processor and process until they are chopped to about the consistency of fine breadcrumbs.

Melt the chocolate by heating in a bowl over boiling water or by microwaving at Medium (50%) power for 2-3 minutes, stirring after every minute. Add the butter and stir until it melts, then add the ground nuts, sugar, vanilla, and milk and mix until well combined. Separate the eggs. Stir the yolks into the hazelnut mixture, and put the whites into another large clean bowl (any traces of fat will prevent the whites fluffing up). Add the salt, then beat the whites until they form stiff peaks.

Sprinkle the flour over the whites, then pour or spoon in the hazelnut mixture and gently fold everything together just enough to combine.

Thoroughly non-stick spray 12 friand or muffin pans (do this carefully because they do have a tendency to stick), and divide the mixture between them.

Bake for 12–15 minutes until the centres spring back when pressed gently. If adding chocolate centres, bake for 4–5 minutes, then (with the tray still in the oven) gently press half to one square (or equivalent) into the top of each friand, and bake for a further 8-10 minutes.

Remove from the oven and leave to cool for 3–5 minutes (this makes them easier to remove), before turning them out of the pans to cool on a rack.

YIELD: 12 friands. **SERVE:** Warm or reheated, with coffee.

slices

Almond Puff Slice

This is an interesting food processor slice for anyone who enjoys making cream puffs!

BASE:

1 cup standard (plain) flour
75g cold butter, cubed
2–4 Tbsp cold water

TOPPING (CHOUX PASTE):

½ cup water
60g butter, cubed
½ cup standard (plain) flour
2 large eggs
½ tsp almond essence

ICING:

2 Tbsp softened butter
2 cups icing sugar
½ tsp almond essence
3 Tbsp hot water
½ cup sliced almonds, lightly toasted

Heat oven to 180°C (170°C fanbake), with the rack just below the middle. While oven heats, toast almonds in one layer in a shallow baking dish.

For pastry, put flour and cold butter (cut into 9 cubes) into the food processor. Pulse to chop butter fairly finely, then add ¾ of the water, a few drops at a time, while pulsing, until the crumbly mixture can be pressed together with your fingers to form a ball of dough. Roll out thinly to 30x30cm on a piece of baking paper, then cut into three 10x30cm strips. Lift the baking paper and pastry onto a baking tray.

For topping, put water and cubed butter in a saucepan. Heat. As soon as it boils and the butter has melted, tip in all the flour. Stir briefly off the heat until dough forms a ball. Transfer hot dough to food processor. Add one egg and almond essence and process until mixed. Beat remaining egg with a fork and add gradually, processing in bursts until mixture is smooth and glossy, and the consistency of spreadable (but not runny) icing.

Spread mixture evenly over the three strips of pastry. Bake for 30–45 minutes. Cool on a rack before drizzling with icing, then sprinkle with the cooled toasted almonds. Cut across the strips into slices of desired size.

For icing, put the softened butter in a bowl. Add the icing sugar and almond essence. Mix with a knife, adding enough water to make icing soft enough to drizzle or spread easily over topping.

SERVE for dessert or with tea or coffee. Best eaten on the day it is made. Store in a shallow, lidded container in a cool place.

Margaret Payne's Neenish Squares

Alison's mother made these rich treats for special occasions! They require some skill and patience but are so good that the effort pays off.

BASE:

100g softened butter
1 cup icing sugar
1 cup standard (plain) flour
½ cup cornflour
milk, if necessary

FILLING:

2 tsp gelatine
2 Tbsp water
100g room temperature butter
1 cup icing sugar
about 4 Tbsp lukewarm water
½–1 tsp rum essence

CHOCOLATE ICING:

2 Tbsp cocoa
4 tsp boiling water
2 Tbsp softened butter
1 cup icing sugar

Heat oven to 170°C (160°C fanbake), with the rack just below the middle of the oven. Line the base and sides of a pan about 18x28cm (see page 94) with baking paper.

For base, beat butter and icing sugar in a bowl (or use a food processor). Rub (or chop) in sifted flour and cornflour until the mixture is the texture of coarse breadcrumbs. Add a little milk if too dry. Spread the crumbly mixture into the baking pan and press it down firmly and evenly. Bake for 15 minutes or until straw coloured. Cool.

For filling, soften gelatine in cold water for 2–3 minutes, then warm to dissolve. Leave to cool.

Cream butter and icing sugar. Beat in lukewarm water a little at a time, stopping if it shows any sign of curdling. Mix in cooled gelatine and essence. If necessary, refrigerate filling until firm but workable, then spread evenly over the base with a knife. Chill again.

For icing, pour boiling water on cocoa in a small bowl. Beat in butter and icing sugar, thinning with cold water if necessary. Spread over chilled filling. Refrigerate for several hours, then cut into small squares.

VARIATION: For a thin base, use half of all ingredients.

SERVE from refrigerator with coffee for a special treat. Store in a shallow, lidded container in the refrigerator for 3–4 days.

Kirsten's Custard Squares

▶

For as long as I can remember, I have had a great weakness for custard squares, so I was delighted when my daughter invented a custard square birthday cake for me.

BASE:
about 200g flaky pastry

FILLING:
½ cup vanilla custard powder
¼ cup brown sugar
2¼ cups milk
2 large eggs
½ tsp vanilla

ICING:
1 cup icing sugar
2 tsp softened butter
lemon juice or passionfruit pulp to mix

Heat oven to 200°C (190°C fanbake), with the rack just below middle of the oven. Line the base and sides of a loose bottomed square 20cm (or 23cm) baking pan (see page 94).

For base, roll the pastry out thinly to make two squares each about 2cm bigger than the pan. Prick the pastry evenly all over. Place the two pastry squares on an oven slide and bake for 7-8 minutes or until golden brown on both sides. Trim the cooked squares of pastry to fit the loose-bottomed baking pan. Place one square in it.

For filling, mix the custard powder and the brown sugar together in a heavy bottomed, medium-sized saucepan. Add the milk and stir until well combined but not foamy. Cook gently over low heat for 2-3 minutes, until the custard thickens. Next, whisk in the beaten (but not foamy) eggs, and the vanilla. Again, stir constantly until the custard thickens, then pour it evenly over the pastry in the baking pan. Cover the hot custard with the other pastry layer immediately. Refrigerate until cold.

For icing, put the icing sugar and butter in a bowl. Stir in small amounts of lemon juice or passionfruit pulp until you get icing of spreadable consistency. Ice the top layer of pastry and leave it to set. Cut into 16 (or 9 larger) squares using a sharp knife.

SERVE from the refrigerator, with coffee or tea, or for dessert. Store squares which are not eaten the day they are made, in the refrigerator, and eat within the next two days.

Walnut Cheesecake Slice

We like this slice served for dessert the day it is made. We cut leftovers into smaller pieces and enjoy them with tea or coffee over the next few days.

BASE:
1 cup standard (plain) flour
¼ cup brown sugar
75g cold butter

FILLING:
1 (250g) carton cream cheese
¼ cup sugar
2 Tbsp brown sugar
1 large egg
½ tsp vanilla
½–¾ cup chopped walnuts

Heat oven to 190°C (180°C fanbake). Place rack in the middle of the oven. Press a large piece of baking paper into a 23cm square pan (see page 94) or a smallish sponge roll pan, folding the paper so it covers the bottom and all sides of the pan. Do not cut the paper at the corners, or filling may run underneath.

For base, rub butter into flour and sugar in a bowl using a pastry blender or fingers until mixture is crumbly (or use a food processor). Press mixture evenly into the lined baking pan. Bake for 10 minutes. While base cooks, make filling.

For filling, soften cream cheese in a bowl with a fork, then add the next four ingredients, and mix until smooth (or re-use unwashed food processor). Pour the cream cheese mixture over the hot, partly cooked base and sprinkle with the finely chopped walnuts.

Bake for 20–30 minutes, or until cream cheese mixture has set in the centre. Cool in pan on a rack. Chill for 2–3 hours before cutting into pieces of the desired size (see page 94).

SERVE larger pieces for dessert with fresh fruit, whipped cream etc. Cut smaller pieces to serve with tea or coffee. Store in a shallow, covered container in refrigerator up to three days.

Coconut Slice

This has been a family favourite for thirty years. Serve warm for dessert or cut in smaller pieces when cold, for a very popular slice. It is easy to make your own pastry in a food processor, but you can use bought pastry if you like.

PASTRY: (SEE NOTE)
1 cup standard (plain) flour
75g cold butter
about ¼ cup cold water

FILLING:
½ cup raspberry jam
about ½ cup currants or sultanas

TOPPING:
175g butter
1½ cups sugar
1 tsp vanilla
3 large eggs
3 cups coconut

Heat oven to 220°C (210°C fanbake), with the rack just below the middle. Spray a 23cm square pan (see page 94) with non-stick spray.

For pastry, put flour and cubed butter in the food processor, then process in bursts, while adding the water in a slow stream. Stop as soon as you can press the dough particles together to make a firm dough. Refrigerate dough 5–10 minutes while you mix the topping.

For topping, soften but do not melt the butter. In the unwashed food processor or bowl, mix butter with the sugar, vanilla and eggs, then mix in the coconut.

Roll out the homemade or bought pastry, so that it is big enough to cover the base and about 1cm up the sides of the pan. Spread it with the jam and dried fruit, then drop the topping over it in blobs, spreading so most of the surface is covered. (Topping will spread during cooking.)

Bake for 10–15 minutes, then turn down to 180°C (170° fanbake) and cook for 15–30 minutes or until the topping has browned evenly, and the centre feels firm.

NOTE: For an extra easy version, replace the homemade pastry with 200g of bought sweet short pastry, or a sheet of pre-rolled pastry. Prick the pastry all over before covering with filling.

SERVE warm for dessert with whipped cream or ice-cream, or cool completely before cutting into pieces of the desired size. Store in a shallow container between layers of paper, in the refrigerator for 3–4 days.

Minted Fruit Squares

Cut this rich slice into small squares. It has a distinctive mint flavour, which is often not recognised because it is unexpected. I imagine that it would keep for several weeks, but in our house, it is always eaten within two or three days!

BASE:
200–250g flaky pastry

FILLING:
1 cup currants
1 cup mixed fruit
½ cup brown sugar
1 cup mint leaves
½ tsp mixed spice
25g softened butter

Heat oven to 190°C (180°C fanbake), with the rack just below the middle. Line the base and sides of a 20cm square baking pan (see page 94) with baking paper.

For base, roll the bought pastry out thinly to form two squares: one 25cm square and one 20cm square. Leave pastry to rest while you mix the filling.

For filling, chop the dried fruit, sugar and mint leaves together, using either a large knife on a large wooden board, or a food processor. (If processing, take care not to overmix, as you don't want to form a paste.) Stir in the spice and the butter, which has been heated until it is soft enough to be mixed evenly through the fruit mixture.

Put the bigger sheet of pastry in the lined baking pan, so that it comes 2cm up the sides, all round, then spread the filling over the base. Cover filling with the smaller sheet of pastry. Dampen the edges of both layers of pastry, then pinch them together to seal. Tidy by trimming or folding edges decoratively. Brush top with milk if desired. Make several small cuts in the pastry so steam can escape during baking.

Bake for 25–35 minutes, until the pastry is evenly brown. Press the pastry down if it has risen unevenly, then leave it to cool completely, before cutting it into 16 small squares with a sharp, serrated knife.

VARIATION: For Fruit Square, leave out the mint altogether.

SERVE at room temperature with tea or coffee. Store in a closed container in the refrigerator or a cool place, for several days (up to a week).

Peanut Butter Squares

These are very popular with children – and often with adults. I like these made thick and cut in small squares so they finish up as cubes.

BASE:

100g butter
½ cup peanut butter
1 cup biscuit crumbs
1 cup icing sugar
about 6 drops almond essence
¼ tsp vanilla

ICING:

½ cup chocolate melts
    or 90g chopped dark chocolate
1 Tbsp peanut butter

Line the base and sides of a pan about 18x28cm (see page 94) with baking paper.

For base, heat the butter (cut into 4 cubes) and peanut butter (in 4-5 blobs) in a large microwave bowl on High (100%) power for 2 minutes or until butter is melted. Take from the microwave and stir until the two are thoroughly blended.

Crumb the (broken) biscuits in a food processor, or put them in a large plastic bag, closing the top loosely with a rubber band. Using a rolling pin, bang and roll the biscuits in the bag until they are crumbed. Add the crumbs, sifted icing sugar and essences to the butter mixture. Mix well, then press into part of the lined baking pan, so that the mixture is 10–15mm high.

For icing, melt the chocolate and soften the peanut butter in a small bowl in the microwave on High (100%) power for 1–2 minutes, just until the two can be mixed together smoothly. Spread over base mixture using a knife. Cool before cutting into small squares with a sharp serrated knife or sharp heavy knife.

SERVE as after dinner treats, with tea, coffee or glasses of milk, or pack in lunches. Store in a covered container (preferably in one layer) in the refrigerator or in a cool place, for up to a week.

Apricot Slice

This slice has a lovely caramel and apricot flavour. Use the larger amount of dried apricots if you can.

100–150g dried apricots
¼ cup orange juice or sherry
75g butter, melted
½ a 400g can sweetened
    condensed milk
½ cup brown sugar
½ cup coconut
1 packet (250g) Wine or Malt biscuits
extra coconut

Line the base and sides of a pan about 18x28cm (see page 94) with baking paper.

Finely chop the dried apricots using kitchen scissors or a sharp knife and cook them in the orange juice or sherry in a large pot until there is no liquid left. Add the butter to the apricots and stir over low heat until melted. Add condensed milk and brown sugar, then heat gently, stirring often until the sugar is no longer grainy, and the mixture is golden brown.

Remove from heat and stir in coconut and the finely crushed biscuits. (To crush the biscuits without a food processor, put them in a large plastic bag, loosely closed with a rubber band, and bang and roll with a rolling pin. Sieve crushed biscuits, crushing any large remaining pieces.) Stir everything together evenly.

Sprinkle the lined baking pan with the extra coconut, then tip in the mixture. Press in evenly to the depth you like (it need not cover the whole tin.) Sprinkle the mixture with more coconut, then refrigerate for at least 2 hours before cutting into pieces of your desired size.

VARIATION: For Apricot & Almond Slice, add ¼–½ plain or lightly toasted, slivered almonds with the crushed biscuits.

SERVE with tea or coffee or pack in lunches. Store in the refrigerator to keep the mixture firm.

Orange Slice

Kirsten learned how to make this, her favourite slice, when she was eight years old! It is now a popular addition to her children's lunch boxes. Replace the orange with other citrus fruit if you like – all are good.

BASE:
100g butter
½ a 400g can sweetened condensed milk
finely grated rind of 1 orange
1 cup desiccated coconut
1 packet (250g) Wine or Malt biscuits

ICING:
25g (2 Tbsp) butter
1 cup icing sugar
about 1 Tbsp orange juice

Line the sides and bottom of a pan about 18x28cm (see page 94) with baking paper.

For base, warm butter in a medium-sized pot or microwave dish until melted. Remove from heat and stir in condensed milk. Finely grate all the coloured rind from an orange. Add the rind and coconut to the butter mixture, then stir until well combined.

Break biscuits into halves or quarters. Put the pieces in a big plastic bag, close bag loosely, and bang and roll the bag with a rolling pin until crumbed, then stir them into the pot. (If you like, crumb the biscuits in a food processor, then add the other ingredients and mix well.)

Press mixture firmly into the lined pan until it is the depth you like (it does not have to cover the whole tin), and level the top.

For icing, put butter in a clean bowl (it should be soft enough to mix easily, but not melted). Add icing sugar and enough juice to mix with a knife so it will spread smoothly over the base. Pattern the icing by making wiggles on top with a fork, then chill until firm. Cut into pieces of the desired size (see page 94).

VARIATION: For Citrus Slice, replace orange rind and juice with rind and juice of other citrus fruit, such as mandarins, lemons, limes etc.

SERVE at any time of day. Good for school lunches and after school snacks. Store in a covered container in the fridge, up to a week, or in the freezer for up to 3 months.

Peppermint Chocolate Squares

Make these to have on hand over the holiday period, or to pack attractively in one layer, in a flat box, to give away as a Christmas gift.

BASE:
125g butter
½ a 400g can sweetened condensed milk
¼ cup sugar
¼ cup cocoa
1 tsp vanilla
1 packet (250g) Wine biscuits

PEPPERMINT ICING:
1 cup icing sugar
1 Tbsp softened butter
1 tsp peppermint essence
2 tsp milk

CHOCOLATE ICING:
50g block cooking chocolate
1 tsp butter

Line the base and sides of a pan about 18x28cm (see page 94) with baking paper.

For base, in a large bowl capable of holding a very hot mixture, microwave the first four ingredients on High (100%) power for about 4 minutes, or until mixture forms a soft ball in cold water. Stir after the first minute. OR: Heat these ingredients in a frypan, stirring frequently, until the mixture has boiled gently for about 2 minutes and forms a soft ball.

Remove from heat and stir in the vanilla. Add crumbed biscuits (crumb biscuits in a food processor or by banging and rolling in a plastic bag with a rolling pin). Mix well. Press mixture evenly into the prepared baking pan.

For peppermint icing, sift or process the icing sugar to remove lumps. Add the room temperature butter and the peppermint essence. Add enough milk to mix a fairly stiff icing, using the food processor or a knife to mix. Spread this on the square.

For chocolate icing, cube the chocolate, and microwave with butter on Medium (50%) power for 2 minutes or until soft enough to spread over the white icing. When chocolate is firm, mark into small (3cm) squares.

VARIATIONS: Replace melted chocolate with chocolate icing, or use 1½ cups icing sugar for more peppermint icing, and leave out the chocolate layer.

SERVE these little squares after dinner with coffee (they tend to disappear from the tin at other times of the day as well). Store in the refrigerator in hot weather.

Chocolate Fudge Squares

This delicious (unbaked) fudge square can be made by quite inexperienced young cooks - show them how, then let them try alone!

BASE:

1 packet (250g) Wine, or Malt or
    Digestive biscuits
½ cup brown sugar
¼ cup cocoa
3 Tbsp milk
75g butter
1 tsp vanilla
1 cup chopped walnuts
    or chopped sultanas
    or a mixture

CHOCOLATE ICING:

1 Tbsp cocoa
2 Tbsp boiling water
1 Tbsp butter
½ tsp vanilla
1 cup icing sugar

Line the sides and bottom of a pan about 18x28cm (see page 94) with baking paper.

For base, crush biscuits in a large plastic bag, fastened loosely with a rubber band, banging and rolling with a rolling pin until quite evenly crushed (or crumb broken biscuits in a food processor without making fine crumbs).

Mix the sugar and cocoa in a fairly large pot or pan, then stir in the milk and add the butter. Bring to the boil, stirring all the time. Take off the heat and stir in the vanilla, crushed biscuits, chopped nuts and/or sultanas.

Press mixture into the lined pan until it is the depth you like (it does not have to cover the whole tin). Flatten surface fairly smoothly with the back of a spoon or fish slice.

For icing, measure the cocoa into a small bowl, add the boiling water and mix to a paste. Add the butter, vanilla and (sifted) icing sugar and beat until smooth (add a little extra water or icing sugar if necessary). Spread on base with a knife and refrigerate until set. Cut into pieces of desired size when firm (see page 94), using a hot, wet knife.

VARIATIONS: To the base and icing, add peppermint essence, OR finely grated tangelo or orange rind, OR rum essence.

SERVE as dessert with coffee, as a mid-afternoon snack, or add to a packed lunch.

Gooey-Chewy Fudge Squares

The name says it all! This square is really a cross between a square and a deliciously chewy candy. Allow time for hardening overnight.

BASE:

75g chilled butter
¼ cup sugar
¾ cup standard (plain) flour

TOPPING:

400g can sweetened condensed
    milk
1 cup dark chocolate melts
    or 180g chopped dark chocolate
¼ tsp rum essence
    or ½ tsp vanilla
¼–½ cup sliced almonds

Heat oven to 170°C (160°C fanbake), with the rack just below the middle. Line the base and sides of a 16x20cm expanding pan (at its smallest) with baking paper (see page 94), folding the lining at the corners so the topping mixture cannot run underneath during cooking.

For base, cut the cold, hard butter into 8–12 cubes and put in a food processor (or grate into a large bowl) with the sugar and flour. Process in bursts, or rub in butter by hand, until the mixture forms small even crumbs. Tip this into the lined baking pan and press down to cover the base evenly. Bake for 10 minutes.

For topping, heat condensed milk and chocolate in a microwave bowl for 2 minutes on High (100%) power, then stir until all the chocolate has melted. Add essence and stir again. Pour over base and sprinkle with sliced almonds.

Bake for 30–45 minutes until you can see that the middle has risen in humps. Cool on a rack, then chill overnight, to allow the topping to firm up, before cutting into fairly small squares.

SERVE with coffee as an after dinner treat. Store in a shallow, lidded container, preferably one layer thick, in a cool place for up to a week.

Butterscotch Squares (from page 78) ▶

Birdseed Bars

Foreground

This sweet bar contains many healthy and flavourful additions. Eat it with restraint – it is all too easy to keep reaching for more!

1 cup sesame seeds
1 cup sunflower seeds
1 cup chopped roasted peanuts
1 cup coconut
  or (fine) rolled oats
  or crushed cornflakes
1 cup sultanas
100g butter
¼ cup honey
½ cup brown sugar

Line the base and sides of a pan about 18x28cm (see page 94) with baking paper.

One variety at a time, watching carefully to prevent over-browning, lightly toast the sesame seeds, sunflower seeds, chopped nuts, coconut, and rolled oats or crushed cornflakes, under a grill or in a large heavy-bottomed frypan on moderate heat. Stir so that the contents brown evenly and lightly. (Do not mix before heating, since they brown at different rates.) Mix them in a large bowl after they are heated, and stir in the sultanas.

Put the butter, honey and brown sugar into the large pan and heat gently until the sugar dissolves, making a toffee-like mixture. Heat until a drop forms a soft ball when dropped in cold water, then tip the toasted ingredients back into the pan. Stir well to combine, then press the mixture into the prepared pan. Leave until lukewarm, then turn out onto a board and, using a sharp serrated knife, cut it into bars the size and shape you like.

VARIATION: Replace peanuts with walnuts or almonds.

SERVE whenever a healthy snack is required. Store promptly when cold, in an airtight container (or carefully wrap pieces individually).

Super Muesli Bars

Background

Muesli bars are really quite easy to make, and homemade bars cost a fraction of the price of bought bars. Toasting the grains first does add an additional step, but gives the bars a delicious nutty flavour.

1 cup (fine) rolled oats
½ cup wheatgerm
½ cup sesame seeds
½ cup sunflower seeds
¼ cup dried apricots, chopped
  (optional)
¼ cup canola or other oil
½ cup honey
¼ cup peanut butter

Line the sides and bottom of a pan about 18x28cm (see page 94) with baking paper, or spray a 23cm square loose bottomed pan.

Mix the first four ingredients together in a sponge roll tin or heavy frypan. Lightly toast the mixture, by cooking about 10cm below a grill or on the stove-top over a medium heat, until it has coloured lightly and lost its raw taste (this should take 5-6 minutes). Stir frequently to ensure nothing burns.

Briefly run the dried apricots under the hot tap, then chop them finely and set aside.

While the oat mixture is browning, measure the oil, honey and peanut butter into a large frypan. Bring to the boil over moderate heat, stirring to blend the ingredients, then turn the heat very low and cook the mixture gently until it forms a soft ball when a little is dropped into cold water and left for about 1 minute.

Stir the lightly browned oat mixture and chopped apricots into the syrup until evenly mixed. Carefully press the hot mixture into prepared pan, using the back of a spoon.

Leave the mixture to cool until firm but still flexible, then turn it out and cut into bars of the desired size (a sharp serrated knife works best for this).

SERVE in school lunches and for after school snacks for teenagers. Store in a completely airtight container, or wrap bars individually in cling wrap. (Like toffee, they soften and turn sticky if left uncovered.)

Pack-A-Snack Bars

This bar makes a popular, concentrated snack food. With its many nutritious additions, it is almost a meal in itself! It carries well in a backpack, school bag or handbag.

BASE:

1 cup standard (plain) flour
1 cup wholemeal flour
1 cup (fine) rolled oats
200g chilled butter
1 cup brown sugar

TOPPING:

4 large eggs
½ cup brown sugar
1 tsp vanilla
2 cups almonds
1 cup dates, chopped
1 cup dried apricots, chopped
1 cup chocolate melts
1 cup desiccated coconut

Heat oven to 180°C (170°C fanbake), with the rack just below the middle of the oven. Line the sides and bottom of a 23cm square pan (see page 94) with baking paper.

For base, chop the flours, oats and cubed butter together in a food processor, or grate the butter into the oats and flours in a bowl. Mix in the brown sugar and press the mixture into the prepared pan. (For a thinner base use half the base ingredients.)

For topping, put eggs, brown sugar and vanilla in a large bowl and beat with a fork just until whites and yolks are evenly mixed. Add all the remaining ingredients and mix together with a stirrer or spatula. Spread over the uncooked base and press down fairly evenly.

Bake for 45 minutes, covering the top with a Teflon liner or folded baking paper if it browns too quickly. Cool in the baking pan, preferably overnight.

When completely cold, cut into four large pieces using a sharp serrated knife. Trim off the outer edges if necessary.

Store pieces in the refrigerator up to a week, or freeze for up to six weeks in plastic bags or covered containers. Cut each piece into bars or fingers as required, just before serving.

Fruit & Nut Bars

If using a food processor, you can make fruit and nut bars which taste much fresher than most bought varieties. The mixture will become firmer on standing, but is never as firm as buttery truffles.

finely grated rind of ½–1 orange
½ cup dried apricots
¼ cup orange juice
½ cup roasted peanuts
½ cup sultanas
½ cup raisins
¼ cup sesame seeds, lightly toasted
½ cup desiccated coconut, lightly toasted
extra coconut for coating

Spray an 18x28cm baking pan (see page 94) with non-stick spray.

Finely grate the orange rind and put aside. Cut the dried apricots in quarters and boil in the orange juice for 5 minutes or until liquid has disappeared.

Put freshly roasted peanuts in the food processor (with the metal chopping blade). Pulse nuts until chopped roughly. Add orange rind, sultanas, raisins, sesame seeds and the softened apricots. Process to the consistency you like. Add coconut and process again. (If mixture is too wet to handle easily, add extra coconut.)

Sprinkle the sprayed baking pan with extra coconut and press in the mixture. Refrigerate uncovered for 24 hours. Cut into rectangular pieces of desired size and coat all surfaces in extra coconut.

NOTE: To toast sesame seeds and coconut, spread thinly in a sponge roll tin and lightly brown under a grill, watching constantly.

SERVE whenever a healthy snack is required! Store in a covered container in the refrigerator up to 3 weeks.

Fudge Brownies

Brownies are traditional American favourites. With their dense, fudgy and slightly chewy texture (and, of course, their delicious chocolate flavour!), they are becoming increasingly popular in New Zealand homes and cafés.

½ cup canola oil and ½ tsp salt
    or 125g butter
1 cup sugar
2 large eggs
1 tsp vanilla
1 cup standard (plain) flour
¼ cup cocoa
1 tsp baking powder
½ cup chopped walnuts (optional)

Heat oven to 180°C (170°C fanbake), with the rack just below the middle. Line the base and sides of a pan about 18x28cm (see page 94) with baking paper.

Measure the oil and salt into a bowl, OR melt the butter in a medium-sized pot or microwave bowl until it is liquid but not hot, then remove from the heat. Beat in (using a fork or stirrer) the sugar, eggs, and vanilla. Sift in the flour, cocoa and baking powder. Add the chopped nuts (if using), and stir until just combined – avoid overmixing. Pour mixture into the lined baking pan and smooth the surface.

Bake for 30 minutes, or until firm in the centre. Mixture will rise up and sink again. The edges will probably be a little higher than the middle, but this does not matter. When cold, cut into pieces of the desired size (see page 94).

SERVE as is, or roll in sifted icing sugar just before serving, covering all surfaces. Brownies do not require icing. Great served as a snack with tea or coffee, or with ice-cream for dessert. Store in an airtight container in a cool place for up to 5 days.

Double Chocolate & Hazelnut Brownies   ▶

Everyone loves brownies! These are moist, chewy and particularly well flavoured.

½ cup canola oil
½ cup white chocolate melts
    or 90g chopped white chocolate
1 cup brown sugar
1 tsp vanilla
2 large eggs
1 cup standard (plain) flour
½ tsp baking powder
½ tsp salt
½–¾ cup lightly roasted hazelnuts,
    roughly chopped
½ cup dark chocolate melts
    or 90g chopped dark chocolate

Heat oven to 180°C (170°C fanbake), with the rack just below the middle. Line the base and sides of a pan about 18x28cm (see page 94) with baking paper.

Combine the oil and white chocolate in a medium-sized pot or microwave bowl. Heat gently, stirring frequently, until the chocolate has melted. Take off heat and cool, then add the sugar, vanilla and eggs and stir until the mixture is smooth.

Sift in the flour, baking powder and salt, and stir gently until evenly mixed. Add the chopped nuts and dark chocolate, and stir until just combined (if the mixture is too warm, the dark chocolate will melt and "marble" the mixture).

Pour into the prepared pan and bake for 25-30 minutes, or until a skewer poked into the centre comes out clean. Cool, then remove from the pan and cut into pieces of the desired size.

VARIATION: Replace hazelnuts with almonds, pecans or macadamias.

SERVE in large pieces with vanilla ice-cream for dessert, or cut into smaller bars to serve with coffee. Store in an airtight container in a cool place for up to 5 days.

Jaffa Nut Brownies

Make these for a treat for yourself, or to give away! Their rich texture makes them very popular. What's more, they are really easy to make. Plain brownies are good, too – for these, just leave out the orange rind and walnuts.

100g butter
75g dark cooking chocolate
2 large eggs
¾ cup sugar
1 tsp vanilla
rind of 1 orange
½ cup chopped walnuts
½ cup standard (plain) flour

Heat oven to 180°C (170°C fanbake), with the rack just below the middle of the oven. Line the base and sides of a 18x28cm pan (see page 94) with baking paper.

Cube butter and break chocolate into pieces. Put both into a microwave bowl and heat for 2 minutes on Medium (50%) power, or warm in a medium-sized pot over low heat, until butter has melted and the chocolate softened. Remove from heat and stir until smooth and combined.

Add eggs, sugar, vanilla, orange rind and chopped nuts and stir until well mixed. Sift in flour and fold together, but do not overmix. Spread the mixture into the lined baking pan.

Bake for about 15 minutes or until the centre feels firm when pressed. (Don't worry if the sides rise more than the centre.) Cool, then cut into pieces of the desired size (see page 94).

SERVE dusted lightly with sieved icing sugar, in larger pieces for dessert with whipped cream or ice-cream, or in smaller pieces with tea or coffee. Store in an airtight container in a cool place, for up to 5 days.

Anne Ford's Churchill Squares

Sam (Simon's wife) has many happy memories of her mother making this for picnics and family gatherings.

FILLING:
1 cup desiccated coconut
2 Tbsp sugar
¾ cup milk

BASE:
100g butter
½ cup sugar
1 large egg
1½ cups standard (plain) flour
2 Tbsp cocoa
1 tsp baking powder

CHOCOLATE ICING:
1 Tbsp cocoa
2 Tbsp boiling water
2 tsp butter
1 cup icing sugar

Heat oven to 180°C (170°C fanbake), with the rack just below the middle. Line the sides and bottom of a pan about 18x28cm (see page 94) with baking paper.

For filling, put the coconut, sugar and milk in a non-stick pan. Heat until sugar dissolves and the milk is soaked up. Take off heat and cool in pan.

For base, beat the softened butter, sugar and egg in a bowl (or use a food processor). Sift in flour, cocoa and baking powder, and mix well. Divide dough in half. Put the baking paper pan-liner on the bench for a size guide, and roll out half the dough on it. Put paper and dough back in pan. Roll remaining dough out on another piece of baking paper the same size.

Spread cool filling evenly on the dough in the pan. Carefully flip remaining dough on top, and lift off baking paper. Pat to neaten edges.

Bake for 20–30 minutes until centre feels firm. Cool on a rack. Ice when cold. Cut into squares of desired size (see page 94), using a sharp serrated knife dipped in hot water.

For icing, pour boiling water on cocoa in a small bowl. Beat in softened butter and icing sugar with a knife. Spread on slice.

SERVE with tea, coffee or milk, or pack in lunches. Store in a closed container in a cool place up to a week.

Lemon Squares

This square has a delicious lemon flavoured custardy topping and always disappears very fast. If you don't have a food processor, you may wish to make another lemon slice instead!

BASE:

2 cups standard (plain) flour
½ cup icing sugar
125g cold butter

TOPPING:

1½ cups sugar
thinly peeled rind of ½ lemon
3 large eggs
¼ cup lemon juice
¼ cup self-raising flour

Heat oven to 160°C (150°C fanbake), with the rack just below the middle. Press a large piece of baking paper into a 23cm square pan (see page 94) or a smallish sponge roll pan, folding the paper so it covers the bottom and all sides. Do not cut the paper at the corners, or filling will run underneath.

For base, measure the flour, icing sugar and cubed butter into a food processor. Process until butter is chopped finely through dry ingredients. Tip mixture into the lined pan and press down firmly and evenly with the back of a large spoon or a fish slice. Bake for 15-20 minutes until firm and straw-coloured. While it cooks, prepare topping.

For topping, put the sugar in the dry, unwashed food processor with the rind peeled from half the lemon (use a potato peeler for this). Process until the rind is very finely chopped through the sugar, then add the eggs, lemon juice and flour, and process until smooth.

Pour over partly cooked base, then bake for about 30 minutes longer, or until top is lightly browned and centre does not wobble when pan is jiggled.

When quite cold, cut into squares or fingers of desired size (see page 94), by pressing a heavy, lightly oiled knife straight down through the topping and base.

SERVE sifted with icing sugar, in large pieces for dessert, with Greek-style yoghurt, lightly whipped cream or marscapone. Serve small pieces with coffee at any time of day. Store lightly covered, up to 3 or 4 days.

Cherry Slice

I worked out this (food processor) recipe after trying a delicious but expensive store-bought slice in London. (It was so good, my sister and I ate our purchase before we left the store!)

BASE:

1 cup standard (plain) flour
¼ cup sugar
100g cold butter

FILLING:

¼–½ cup chopped crystallised
   cherries
½ cup raspberry jam

TOPPING:

1½ cups desiccated coconut
1 cup sugar
½ cup standard (plain) flour
½ cup flaked almonds (optional)
50g cold butter
2 large eggs
¼–½ tsp almond essence

Heat oven to 180°C (170°C fanbake), with the rack just below the middle. Spray a 23cm square loose bottomed pan with non-stick spray (see page 94).

For base, put the flour, sugar and very cold butter (in 9 cubes), in the food processor bowl. Process until butter is cut into very small crumbs, then press the mixture flat in the prepared pan with the back of a spoon or a fish slice. Bake for 15 minutes. While it bakes, prepare the filling, chopping the cherries fairly finely. Set aside.

For topping, combine first four ingredients in the unwashed food processor bowl. Add the butter, cut in nine cubes, then process until butter is cut through the mixture. Add the eggs and essence and blend until well mixed.

Take the partly cooked base from the oven.

For filling, spread warm base with jam, then sprinkle evenly with cherries.

Using two teaspoons, carefully drop the topping mixture over the filling. Spread topping lightly, to cover the jam and cherries without mixing the layers.

Bake for 20–30 minutes longer, until lightly browned and firm when touched. Cool on a rack. When cold, cut into pieces of desired size (see page 94).

SERVE large pieces, warm, for dessert, and smaller pieces, cold, with tea, coffee etc. Refrigerate in a covered container, between layers of baking paper, up to a week. Freeze for longer storage.

Marjie's Lemon Shortcake ▶

As we devour this particularly delicious treat, we always think about the friend who was kind enough to give us her recipe. Sharing recipes with friends, over the years, is a tradition we treasure.

BASE & TOPPING:

1 cup self-raising flour
1 cup standard (plain) flour
1 cup sugar
100g cold butter
1 large egg, lightly beaten
2 Tbsp milk

FILLING:

100g butter
2 lemons, grated rind and juice
1 cup sugar
2 large eggs, lightly beaten

Heat oven to 180°C (170°C fanbake), with rack just below the middle. Line the base and sides of a 23cm square loose bottomed cake pan (see page 94) with baking paper.

For base, mix the sifted flours and sugar in a bowl. Grate in the cold butter, then rub it in until it looks like rolled oats (or chop in butter cubes in a food processor). Make a well in the centre and add the lightly beaten egg. Add just enough milk so that particles will stick together when pressed, making a dough. Press half this over bottom of pan, keeping the rest to crumble on top.

For filling, melt butter in a medium-sized pot. Take off heat. Beat in the grated lemon rind and juice, sugar and eggs, then heat again, stirring constantly, until mixture thickens to a pouring custard. Take off heat as soon as first bubbles form. Pour it evenly over the base and crumble remaining dough mixture on top.

Bake for 35–45 minutes, until golden brown, with centre almost as firm as the edges. Remove from loose bottomed pan. When cool, dust with icing sugar.

SERVE large pieces warm for dessert, with whipped cream or ice-cream. Also delicious served cold in smaller pieces with tea or coffee. Store in a single layer in a loosely covered container, or refrigerate in an airtight container for longer.

Butterscotch Squares

Alison simplified a three-layered butterscotch bar for "beginner" cooks, and it remains enormously popular!

BASE & TOPPING:

125g butter
½ cup sugar
1 large egg
1 tsp vanilla
1 cup self-raising flour
1 cup standard (plain) flour

FILLING:

100g butter
2 rounded household Tbsp golden syrup
400g can sweetened condensed milk

Heat oven to 180°C (170°C fanbake), with the rack just below the middle. Line a 23cm square baking pan (see page 94) with 2 strips of baking paper, so bottom and all sides are covered.

For base, cut butter into 9 pieces and warm in a large pot or microwave dish until it starts to melt. Take off heat and beat in the sugar, egg and vanilla with a fork or stirrer, until evenly mixed. Stir in the flours until mixture is crumbly, then squeeze it into a ball with your hands. Break ¾ of the dough into bits, and place these evenly in the prepared baking pan, patting them fairly flat. (You can put a piece of plastic between the mixture and your fingers if you like.) Put the rest of the dough in the refrigerator or freezer.

For filling, melt the butter in a pot or microwave-proof bowl. Measure the syrup, using a hot wet spoon, and stir in. Add the condensed milk, mix well, then pour the filling over the unbaked mixture in the tin.

For topping, coarsely grate the (cold) remaining piece of dough on top of the filling, using a grater with large holes. Bake for 30–45 minutes, until the crust is golden and the filling has browned. Cool on a rack for 2 hours, then lift carefully from the baking pan (on the paper) and cut into pieces of desired size (see page 94), using a sharp knife dipped in hot water.

SERVE any time, with tea, coffee or milk, or pack in lunches. Store in a covered container, refrigerating if keeping for a week or so, or freezing for longer storage.

(See photograph on page 67.)

Lindsay's Christmas Mincemeat Squares

These are far quicker to make than Christmas Mincemeat Pies, and they are just as popular. They are best eaten within a few days – but believe me, you won't find this a problem!

BASE:
100g chilled butter
½ cup (packed) brown sugar
1 cup standard (plain) flour

TOPPING:
1 cup (packed) brown sugar
¼ cup plain flour
½ tsp baking powder
½ tsp salt
1 cup desiccated coconut
2 large eggs
1 tsp vanilla
1 cup (280–300g) fruit mince

Heat oven to 160°C (150°C fanbake), with the rack just below the middle. Line the base and sides of a pan about 18x28cm (see page 94) with baking paper.

For base, cut the cold butter into 8–12 cubes and put in a food processor (or grate it into a large bowl) with the brown sugar and flour. Process in bursts, or rub in butter by hand, until it is evenly through the flour, and mixture is crumbly. Tip this mixture into the prepared pan and press it down so it covers the base evenly. Bake for 10 minutes.

For topping, measure all the dry ingredients into the unwashed food processor or large bowl and mix well. Add the eggs, vanilla and homemade or bought fruit mince and process or beat until everything is well blended. Pour on top of the cold, warm or hot base and bake for about 30 minutes, until centre of topping feels firm and has browned evenly.

Cool thoroughly before cutting into small squares or bars.

SERVE squares at any festive occasion, with wine, cocktails or coffee, or warm them and serve for dessert, cut in larger pieces, with vanilla ice-cream or lightly whipped cream and a fresh berry garnish. Store in a shallow container (preferably one layer deep) in a cool place with lid slightly ajar.

Walnut, Date & Ginger Slice

This slice contains a satisfying mixture of dried fruit, nuts and crystallised ginger, topped with a delicious Ginger Crunch-like icing.

BASE:
2 cups chopped dates
½ cup chopped crystallised ginger
½ cup water
1 cup chopped walnuts
125g softened butter
1 cup brown sugar
2 large eggs
1 tsp vanilla
1½ cups standard (plain) flour
½ cup (fine) rolled oats
2 tsp baking powder

ICING:
2 Tbsp butter
2–3 tsp ground ginger
2 rounded household Tbsp golden syrup
2 cups icing sugar
about 2 tsp water

Heat oven to 180°C (170°C fanbake), with the rack just below the middle. Line the base and sides of a 23cm square pan (preferably loose bottomed) with baking paper (see page 94).

For base, chop each date and piece of ginger into three or four pieces. Put in a covered non-stick pan with the water. Stand over high heat until water boils rapidly. Stir fruit carefully after 2 minutes, then leave the lid off until water evaporates. Take pan off heat and stand in cold water. Stir in chopped walnuts.

Mix butter and sugar thoroughly in a food processor or bowl. Beat in the eggs and vanilla, then add the dry ingredients and mix until combined. Tip mixture from processor or bowl into the pan with the cooked mixture. Stir to mix, then pour into the prepared baking pan. Bake for about 30 minutes, until a skewer in the centre comes out clean.

For icing, warm the butter, ginger and golden syrup in the frypan until melted. (Do not boil.) Take off heat. Add the sifted icing sugar and beat well with a fork or wooden spoon until smooth, adding enough water to make a spreadable consistency. Ice while slice is warm (but not hot). Decorate with extra sliced ginger and walnuts if desired and, when icing is set, cut into fingers with a sharp knife.

VARIATION: Leave out ginger from slice and icing, if desired.

SERVE any time with tea or coffee, or add to packed lunches. Store in a shallow, lidded container in a cool place for 3–4 days.

Louise Cake

A favourite café slice, this is not hard to make.

BASE:

100g softened butter
½ cup sugar
2 (large) egg yolks
1 tsp vanilla
1 cup self-raising flour
1 cup standard (plain) flour

FILLING:

½ cup good quality raspberry jam

TOPPING:

2 large egg whites
1 tsp vanilla
½ cup sugar
¾ cup coconut shreds

Heat oven to 160°C (150°C fanbake), with the rack just below the middle of the oven. Line the sides and bottom of a pan about 18x28cm (see page 94) with baking paper, allowing enough extra paper on the sides for lifting the cooked slice out, or spray a 23cm square loose bottomed pan.

For base, put the softened butter and sugar in a food processor or large bowl. Separate two eggs, adding the yolks to this mixture (and put the whites in a very clean medium-sized bowl ready to use for the topping). Add the vanilla, mix the egg yolks through the softened butter and sugar, then add the two flours and mix again until evenly crumbly. Tip crumbly mixture into prepared pan and press down evenly. Bake for 15 minutes.

Make topping while base cooks. Beat the egg whites and vanilla until frothy, then add the sugar and beat until the tips of peaks turn over when the beater is lifted from them. Fold the coconut evenly through the meringue.

For filling, spread the jam over the hot, partly cooked shortcake.

Put the meringue in spoonfuls over jam, then spread evenly with a knife. Sprinkle with 2 tablespoons of extra coconut if you like. Bake for about 15 minutes or until the meringue feels crisp and is evenly and lightly coloured.

Cool completely before cutting into pieces of the desired size.

SERVE with tea or coffee. Store preferably one layer deep in a cool place, with lid slightly ajar.

Spicy Fruit Slice

This slice has an irresistible combination of textures and flavours.

BASE:

125g butter, softened
½ cup sugar
1 large egg
2 cups standard (plain) flour
2 tsp baking powder
1 tsp mixed spice
1 tsp cinnamon

FILLING:

2 Tbsp sugar
¼ cup apricot jam
¼ cup coconut
¼ cup currants
25g butter
1 large egg, beaten
rind and juice of 1 lemon

ICING:

1 Tbsp butter, softened
finely grated rind of ½ lemon
1 cup icing sugar
3–4 tsp lemon juice

Heat oven to 180°C (170°C fanbake). Place rack in the middle of the oven. Line the base and sides of a pan about 18x28cm (see page 94) with baking paper, or spray a 20cm square loose bottomed pan.

For base, cream butter and sugar, add the egg and mix again, then add the sifted dry ingredients (or mix in a food processor). Divide the mixture in two and press one half into the baking pan. Roll the other half out the same size, on a piece of plastic, and put aside.

For filling, heat sugar, jam, coconut, currants and butter until the mixture boils. Cool the container in cold water, then beat in the egg, finely grated lemon rind and juice, with a fork. Spread this mixture over the base, cover with remaining dough, and lift away the plastic, pressing gently into the corners.

Bake for 25–30 minutes, until the centre springs back when lightly pressed.

For (optional) icing, beat together butter, lemon rind and sifted icing sugar in a small bowl. Add lemon juice 1 teaspoon at a time until creamy. Spread on cooled slice, making wavy patterns with a fork. Leave to set.

SERVE cut into fingers of desired size. Store between layers of paper in a closed container in a cool place for up to a week.

Ginger Crunch

Ginger Crunch is another perennial family favourite; even though it seems to have been around forever, it is still popular.

BASE:

125g butter
¼ cup sugar
1 tsp baking powder
1 cup standard (plain) flour
1 tsp ground ginger

ICING:

2 Tbsp butter
2 tsp ground ginger
2 rounded household Tbsp golden syrup
1 Tbsp water
2 cups icing sugar

Heat oven to 180°C (170°C fanbake), with the rack just below the middle. Line the sides and bottom of a pan about 18x28cm (see page 94) with baking paper, allowing extra on the sides for lifting out the cooked slice, or spray a 23cm square loose bottomed pan.

For base, cut the cold butter into 9 cubes, then process in brief bursts with remaining base ingredients, until the mixture is the texture of coarse breadcrumbs. If mixing by hand, warm butter until soft, mix it with the sugar, then stir in the sieved dry ingredients. Press the crumbly mixture into the pan firmly and evenly.

Bake for about 10 minutes or until evenly and lightly browned. While hot, it will still feel soft. While the base cooks make the icing, since the base should be iced while hot.

For icing, measure the butter, ginger, golden syrup and water into a small pot or microwave bowl. Heat, without boiling, until melted. Take off heat, sift in the icing sugar, and beat until smooth. When the base is cooked, take it from the oven, pour the warm icing onto the hot base and spread carefully so it covers the base evenly. Leave to cool and set. Do not take from the pan until it has cooled completely.

NOTE: For a really thick icing, use one and a half times the icing recipe!

VARIATION: Sprinkle partly set icing with ½–1 cup chopped nuts of your choice.

SERVE with tea or coffee, or pack in lunches. Store in a cool place up to a week.

Chocolate Caramel Bars

Sometimes, when somebody goes out to buy the ingredients we need for our next cooking project, they come back with a small treat from a nearby baker's shop! When you make these yourself, you get a whole batch for the same price as two bought pieces!

BASE:

100g softened butter
¼ cup castor sugar
1 cup standard (plain) flour

FILLING:

100g butter
½ a 400g can sweetened condensed milk
½ cup golden syrup
¼ cup chopped walnuts (optional)

ICING:

1 Tbsp cocoa
1½ Tbsp boiling water
2 tsp softened butter
¼ tsp vanilla
1 cup icing sugar

Heat oven to 170°C (160°C fanbake), with the rack just below the middle. Line the base and sides of a pan about 18x28cm (see page 94) with baking paper.

For base, cream the soft butter and castor sugar, then stir in flour. Press into prepared baking pan.

Bake for 6–8 minutes or until the centre is firm. Do not overcook, or your bars will be very hard to cut later.

For filling, measure butter, condensed milk and golden syrup into a pot. Bring to the boil over medium heat, stirring all the time, then reduce heat and cook for 10 minutes, stirring often, until the mixture is a deep golden colour, and a drop of it forms a soft ball in cold water.

Take off heat, stir in chopped walnuts (if using), and pour over cooked base straight away, smoothing out if necessary. Leave to cool before icing.

For icing, pour boiling water on cocoa in a small bowl. Beat in butter, vanilla and sifted icing sugar, adding more water if necessary, to make icing soft enough to spread easily over the caramel.

Leave uncovered for at least 2 hours before cutting into bars.

SERVE with tea or coffee, or as an after dinner treat.

Belgian Bars

This spicy mixture spreads an enticing smell through the house as it bakes. All age groups love it!

BASE:

1 cup brown sugar, packed
200g softened butter
1 large egg
1 tsp cinnamon
2 tsp mixed spice
4 tsp baking powder
2 cups standard (plain) flour

FILLING:

about ½ cup raspberry jam

ICING:

2 cups sifted icing sugar
25g softened butter
about 3 Tbsp lemon juice or water
red jelly crystals (or coloured sugar*)

Heat oven to 160°C (150°C fanbake), with the rack just below the middle. Line the base and sides of a large sponge roll pan (see page 94) with baking paper.

For base, measure the brown sugar, softened butter and egg into a large bowl (or a food processor). Mix well, then add all the dry ingredients except the flour. Mix again, then add and mix in half the flour. Add remaining flour and mix well.

Divide dough into two parts, and refrigerate in a plastic bag until firm enough to roll. Roll each half out to fit your baking pan. (If you like, work with the dough between sheets of floured, waxed paper or plastic to prevent sticking.)

Place the first sheet in the prepared baking pan and neaten the edges. Spread it with a thin layer of jam, then cover with the second sheet of dough. Prick in a few places.

Bake for 20-30 minutes until the centre is firm when gently pressed. Cool, ice as below and cut into bars.

For icing (if desired), mix icing sugar, butter and enough lemon juice or water to make a fairly soft icing. Spread evenly over the cooked mixture. If you like, sprinkle a few red jelly crystals (or some coloured sugar*) on the icing.

* Coloured sugar: Add a few drops of cochineal to 2 tablespoons of sugar and mix until evenly coloured. Dry before use.

SERVE with tea or coffee. Store bars in airtight jars in a cool place for about a week, if they get the chance!

Chocolate Surprise Bars

This delicious slice forms a jelly-like central layer as it bakes. Leave it overnight before cutting it into bars.

BASE:

100g chilled butter
½ cup sugar
1 cup standard (plain) flour

FILLING:

2 large or 3 small eggs
1 tsp vanilla
1½ cups brown sugar
1 cup desiccated coconut
¼ cup standard (plain) flour
2 Tbsp cocoa
½ cup dark chocolate melts
    or 90g chopped dark chocolate
1 tsp baking powder
¼ tsp salt
1½ cups grated, squeezed zucchini

TOPPING:

½ cup dark chocolate melts

Heat oven to 160°C (150°C fanbake), with the rack just below the middle. Line the base and sides of a pan about 18x28cm (see page 94) with baking paper, folding it at the corners so the topping mixture cannot run underneath during cooking.

For base, put the cold cubed butter in a food processor (or grate it into a large bowl) with the sugar and flour. Process in bursts, or rub in butter by hand, forming small, even crumbs. Tip the crumbly mixture into the prepared pan and press down firmly and evenly. Bake for 10 minutes.

For filling, mix the first 3 ingredients well in the unwashed food processor or a bowl. Mix everything else (except zucchini) in another bowl. Grate, squeeze, then measure the unpeeled zucchini. Toss with the other ingredients, then add to the egg mixture. Process briefly, or stir together, then pour over partly baked base.

For topping, sprinkle chocolate melts over the surface.

Bake for 45 minutes or until the centre feels firm. Cool overnight before cutting into bars or squares of desired size (see page 94).

SERVE as a treat at any time of the day. Store in one layer in a shallow, lidded container in the refrigerator, for up to 5 days.

Spiced Fruit Shortcake

This plain shortcake has an interesting spicy filling. It may be made ahead and frozen in one large piece or individual squares, if desired.

FILLING:

½ cup sultanas, raisins or currants
½ cup chopped dried apricots
½ cup brown sugar
2 tsp mixed spice
½ tsp ground cloves
½ cup orange juice
1 Tbsp balsamic or wine vinegar
3 large apples, peeled and cubed
about 1 Tbsp custard powder

BASE & TOPPING:

125g softened butter
½ cup sugar
1 large egg
2¼ cups standard (plain) flour
2 tsp baking powder

Heat oven to 180°C (170°C fanbake), with the rack just below the middle. Line the base and sides of a 23cm square loose bottomed baking pan (see page 94) with baking paper.

For filling, mix the sultanas, apricots, sugar, spice and cloves together in a frypan. Add the orange juice, vinegar and the apple cubes. Cover and simmer for 2-3 minutes, then thicken with the custard powder (which you have mixed to a paste with a little cold water), until filling is thick enough to keep its shape. Remove from heat and cool to room temperature.

For base and topping, beat the soft butter, sugar and egg until light and creamy, then mix in the sifted dry ingredients, making a soft dough. Cut the dough in half and chill half in refrigerator or freezer. Pat out the other piece of dough on the baking paper to fit the bottom of the pan, using enough extra flour to stop it sticking.

Spread the thickened, cooled filling on the base. Roll out the other half of the dough and place on top of filling, or grate coarsely over the top. (The grated topping flattens as the shortcake cooks.)

Bake for 30–45 minutes, until centre feels firm. Sprinkle with icing sugar.

VARIATION: Replace fresh apple with two 380g cans of diced apple.

SERVE warm in large pieces, with whipped cream or ice-cream, or refrigerate smaller pieces to eat cold, over the next three days. If desired, freeze for up to a month.

Spicy Apple Shortcake

Plain apple is sandwiched between two layers of a deliciously spicy crust in this very popular shortcake.

FILLING:

567g can apple slices or 3 cups well-drained chunky pieces of stewed apple*

CRUST:

125g softened butter
¾ cup plain or brown sugar
1 large egg
2¼ cups standard (plain) flour
2 tsp baking powder
¼ cup cocoa
1 tsp cinnamon
1 tsp mixed spice
¼ tsp ground cloves (optional)

* If preparing fresh apple, peel, chop and cook the apple in a small amount of water until it is barely tender, then drain in a sieve. Measure the 3 cups after cooking and draining. Cool to room temperature.

Heat oven to 180°C (170°C fanbake), with the rack just below the middle. Line the base and sides of a 23cm square, preferably loose-bottomed baking pan (see page 94) with baking paper.

For filling, open canned apple, drain, then chop into smaller, evenly sized chunks.

For base and topping, beat the soft butter and sugar together in a bowl or food processor, then add the egg and beat again. Sift in the remaining ingredients and mix to make quite a soft dough. Halve the dough and chill half in the refrigerator or freezer. Pat or roll out the other half on the paper pan-lining, using extra flour to prevent sticking if you need to.

Spread the drained apple evenly over the base, then coarsely grate the remaining chilled dough over the apple. (The grated topping will spread and flatten as it cooks.)

Bake for 30–45 minutes, or until the centre feels firm. Sprinkle with icing sugar before cutting.

SERVE, refrigerate and freeze as for Spiced Fruit Shortcake.

Making Delicious Muffins

Please take a few minutes to read these pages before you make the recipes in this book, even if you already make muffins. To work really efficiently, and to make your reputation as an expert muffin maker, it helps to know all the finer points! Remember though, that these are general instructions, and that there are exceptions to every rule!

Before you start measuring and mixing, turn on the oven so it is up to heat before your muffins go into it. Try to measure dry ingredients before wet ones, since this eliminates washing and drying measuring spoons and cups part way through the measuring.

For greatest efficiency, measure the liquids into a large bowl, and add the (mixed) dry ingredients to them later. You can then simply dust off the container in which the dry ingredients were combined, without washing it, saving a little extra time and effort!

Unless you are using self-raising flour as the only dry ingredient, combine the dry ingredients in a dry bowl (or other container) big enough to mix them in. Sifting or sieving them is unnecessary if you toss or whisk them with a dry whisk or fork once they are in the bowl. Mix them well, so they are light, airy, and well combined. This is important, since later mixing should be minimal.

Next, measure and mix all the liquid ingredients together. Most of the time, we mix these in a large bowl. When you use oil instead of butter, combining the liquids is easier, since you do not need to melt the butter first. If you are adding heated ingredients to liquid mixtures, try to cool them so that your final liquid mixture is not warm. If it is, your muffins may rise in the bowl rather than in the oven.

Sometimes it is easier to mix liquid ingredients in a food processor. When we do this, we tip the processed liquids into the dry ingredients in a large bowl. Follow the recipe instructions.

Nuts are a good addition to healthy muffins. You can always add ¼–½ cup of chopped nuts without altering the recipe in other ways. Add chopped walnuts to liquid ingredients so unmixed flour does not stick in their crannies!

In general, add sugar to dry ingredients, because it makes the dry ingredients easier to fold into the wet ingredients.

The way you combine the dry and wet mixtures is vital. Always tip ALL the dry ingredients into the wet ones (or vice versa) at once. FOLD THEM TOGETHER WITH AS LITTLE MIXING AS POSSIBLE, without stirring or beating. NEVER use a whisk at this stage. A flexible straight-bladed spreader/scraper does by far the best job. (See mail order details on page 96.) Slowly bring your spreader/scraper, fork or spoon down the side of the bowl and under the mixture, then up through it, turning bowl and repeating this until no pockets of flour are left. Stop while the mixture looks rough and lumpy. NEVER give it a quick beat or stir for good measure!

Occasionally a muffin mixture may seem too dry, since ingredients sometimes vary in wetness. With experience, you can notice dryness before you finish mixing. Add 1–2 tablespoons of milk, juice or water straight away, folding it in as little as necessary, until the consistency seems right. If you do this too late, you run the risk of over-mixing, and will get peaked, tough muffins.

Muffins, especially the low-fat variety, can stick like crazy! Use pans with a non-stick finish, clean these well, but without scratching them, and always use a light, even coating of non-stick spray as well.

Spoon muffins into prepared pans, helping the mixture off with another spoon, rather than letting it drop off by itself. Try to divide the mixture evenly – put as few spoonfuls in each pan as possible. Let the mixture mound naturally – do not smooth or interfere with its surface. Add toppings (page 92/93) to ANY muffins, for extra interest, if you like.

Bake muffins nearly always in the centre of the oven, until the centres spring back when pressed. If this is hard to judge, especially if the muffin contains "lumpy" additions, push a skewer into the centre. When it comes out clean, the muffins are ready. Cooking times are only a guide. Ovens vary in temperature. If your muffins are too pale when they are cooked, raise the temperature 10 degrees next time. If they are too dark, lower the temperature next time.

Let cooked muffins stand in their pans for 3–4 minutes. Like magic, they stop sticking in this time! Press down gently on the edges of a muffin with several fingers of one hand, and twist slightly. As soon as the muffin will turn freely, lift it out, and let it finish cooling on a rack. Very small rubber scrapers help remove muffins from pans too.

Most muffins are best served warm, soon after baking. They will stay warm for some time, without going soggy, in a napkin-lined basket. Reheat (without overheating) in a microwave oven, or in a paper bag at about 150°C in a conventional oven.

Low-fat muffins dry out faster than richer ones. To retard this, put them in plastic bags as soon as they are cold. Freeze muffins you do not think you will eat within a day or two at this stage, too. When practical, warm thawed muffins before serving them. Frozen muffins in packed lunches are useful for keeping other foods cold, too.

Modifying Existing Muffin Recipes

There may be times when you want to make changes, substitutions or additions to your favourite muffin recipes, to suit special dietary requirements, to fit in with your own personal eating pattern or to use ingredients you have on hand. We hope that the following guidelines, explanations and suggestions will help you.

Wholemeal flour

Research shows that most of us would benefit by eating more fibre, so using more wholemeal flour when baking is a step in the right direction. Replacing up to half the regular (white) flour in a muffin recipe with wholemeal will usually make little noticeable difference to the finished muffins. Simply substitute up to half the regular (white) flour with wholemeal flour, or half the white self-raising flour with self-raising wholemeal, adding an extra tablespoon of liquid for each cup of wholemeal used.

Low cholesterol muffins

Replace 1 large egg with the whites of 2 large eggs. Use canola or light olive oil, or an olive, avocado or canola oil-based spread in place of butter, replacing 50g butter with ¼ cup of oil. (You may want to add a little extra salt when replacing butter with oil). In many 2 egg muffin recipes you can leave out 1 egg altogether, and add 2-4 Tbsp of extra liquid instead.

Lower fat muffins

The butter or oil content of most muffin recipes can be reduced by half (or even more) by adding an equal volume of plain low-fat yoghurt or fruit purée in its place. The texture will not be exactly the same and the muffins should be eaten the day they are made, for best results.

For further fat reductions use low-fat milks (or non-fat dried milk and water) in place of regular milk, and other reduced fat dairy products (like 98% fat-free Sour Cream) in place of their full fat cousins.

Lower fat cheesy muffins

We bake cheese muffins at a high temperature to get an appetising golden-brown coloured crust and a good flavour. Replace grated cheese with quarter to half as much Parmesan for a definite cheese flavour but less fat. Muffins that contain large amounts of cheddar cheese do not need added butter or oil as well.

Non-dairy muffins

Use soy milk instead of milk, and soy yoghurt in place of yoghurt or sour cream. Replace butter with the same amount of dairy-free margarine or with oil. When using oil replace 50g butter with ¼ cup of oil, and add a little (¼ tsp) salt.

Golden Rules for Marvellous Muffins Each Time.

- Turn on the oven before you start mixing

- Measure carefully, using standard, level cup and spoon measures

- Too much flour makes dry muffins – never pack or "bang" it into cup measures

- Always mix dry ingredients thoroughly before adding liquid mixture

- Mix all liquids together before adding them (all at once) to the dry mixture

- NEVER OVERMIX MUFFINS! FOLD WET AND DRY MIXTURES TOGETHER UNTIL JUST COMBINED – MIXTURE SHOULD NOT BE SMOOTH

- It's OK to see a little dry flour but not pockets of it

- Cook muffins in non-stick pans using non-stick spray

- For maximum moistness cook muffins at high heat for a short time

- Muffins are cooked as soon as centres spring back when pressed

- Muffins should come out cleanly if cooled in pans for 3-4 minutes before removal

- Muffins are best eaten while warm (or reheated)

- Bag muffins as soon as cool to prevent drying out

More About Muffins…

Muffin Sizes

You can buy muffin pans of varying sizes. Whatever you buy, make sure it has a good non-stick finish, since many muffin mixtures stick badly!

We usually use regular-sized muffin pans, but sometimes it is nice to try something different. Children particularly like sweet mini muffins, while savoury mini muffins make great nibbles to serve with drinks.

Large "Texan" muffins can also be good if you are serving a savoury muffin as part of a meal (i.e. with soup or a salad). If you are watching your waist, we suggest that you avoid them, since they are twice the size of a regular muffin.

Regular-sized Muffins

Most widely used are muffin trays which make twelve muffins. (The twelve depressions, if filled with water, hold 4 cupfuls altogether.) Most of the recipes in this book will make 12 muffins this size. We spoon about quarter of a cup of mixture into each muffin hole.

You can also buy muffin trays with six holes the size of those above. These fit in some bench-top ovens, and are also handy if you have a little mixture left over, and want to make a few more muffins.

We have recently also experimented with flexible silicon muffin trays. These worked well, although the bottoms and sides of the muffins don't brown in quite the same way.

Mini Muffins

Mini muffin tins are fun! Hardly anyone will refuse one of these little muffins which are a little less than half the size of those above. (A muffin tray holding 12 mini muffins, if filled with water, holds 1 cupful.) A mixture making 12 regular muffins will make 24-30 mini muffins. Mini muffins usually need about two minutes shorter baking time than regular muffins.

Mini muffin trays usually fit in bench-top ovens.

Texan Muffins

These large muffins are made in trays of six. Each muffin is twice the size of a regular muffin. Muffins from these trays always look extra-generous. (The tray of six holds 5 cups of water altogether.) These muffins usually take 2-4 minutes longer to cook than regular muffins.

Gem Irons

If you have gem irons tucked away in a bottom cupboard, by all means try cooking your muffins in them. Heat the irons in the oven as it warms up. Put the hot irons on a heat-resistant surface, spray well with non-stick spray, then drop in the mixture from the SIDE of a dessertspoon. The cooking time will be shorter than for regular muffins.

Paper Cases

Paper cases the size of regular muffin pans are sometimes used for muffins which are to be sold or handled a lot. Paper cases are helpful for microwaved muffins which otherwise stick to their plastic pans.

Toppings for Marvellous Muffins

Add extra appeal to your muffins with interesting toppings and spreads.

Toppings for Sweet and Bran Muffins

Before cooking: Top with Cinnamon Sugar, Streusel Topping, Sesame Sugar, chopped walnuts, almonds, or cashews, sunflower, pumpkin, poppy or sesame seeds or chocolate chips.

Cinnamon Sugar: Shake together in a screw-topped jar ¼ cup of brown sugar, ¼ cup of white sugar, and 1 Tbsp of cinnamon. Sprinkle ½–1 tsp over each muffin before baking.

Streusel Topping: Chop until crumbly, in a food processor or bowl, 1 Tbsp each of cold butter and flour, 2 Tbsp each of sugar and chopped nuts, and ½ tsp of cinnamon. Sprinkle this amount onto 12 regular sweet or bran muffins before baking them.

Sesame Sugar: Grind 2 Tbsp toasted sesame seeds using a pestle and mortar or a coffee grinder. Add 2 Tbsp each brown sugar and white sugar, and a pinch of salt. Mix or grind briefly. Store in an airtight jar in a cool place. Sprinkle about a teaspoonful over any sweet or bran muffin before baking.

After cooking: Dust with icing sugar or top with crunchy lemon glaze (page 18), lemon glaze (page 28), ginger glaze (page 33), or Icing to Drizzle. Split muffins and fill or top with cottage cheese, cream cheese, quark, or bought toppings, or make Rum Butter (Alison's favourite) or Brandy Butter.

Icing to Drizzle: Sieve ¼ cup icing sugar, and add, to make a smooth, pourable cream, 1–2 tsp of water, lemon or orange juice, etc. For a "generous drizzle", double these quantities. Pour over hot or warm, not cold, muffins.

Rum Butter: Beat or process together 100g softened butter, 1 cup brown sugar, 1 tsp freshly grated nutmeg, and 2 Tbsp rum, until light and creamy. Serve at room temperature. (This is wonderful with any sweet or bran muffin.)

Brandy Butter: Replace the rum with brandy in the recipe above, and leave out the nutmeg.

Toppings for Savoury Muffins

Before cooking: Put grated cheese, cubes of cheese, shreds of Parmesan, toasted sesame seeds, poppy seeds, pumpkin seeds, sunflower seeds, paprika, cayenne and chilli powder on savoury muffins.

After cooking: Split muffins (sometimes from top to bottom, at other times from side to side) and use interesting spreads.

Buy: Cream cheese, cottage cheese, savoury cottage cheese, etc.

Make: Horseradish cream cheese, herb butters.

At times: Sandwich the two halves of mini muffins, or top halved regular muffins with thin slices of ham, pastrami, smoked pork, beef or lamb, smoked salmon, mussels, luncheon sausage etc., depending on the occasion. Add sliced tomatoes, cucumber pickles, salad vegetables, etc.

Horseradish Cream Cheese: Mix together ¼ cup cream cheese and 1 Tbsp (bottled) grated horseradish or fresh grated horseradish to taste.

Herb Butter: Food process or mix 100g softened butter and ½–1 cup of chopped fresh herbs. Add ¼–½ cup finely grated Parmesan cheese if you like.

Measures for Muffins & Slices

For consistently good results when you use the recipes in this book, please measure the ingredients carefully.

Most recipe ingredients have been measured rather than weighed, and the quantities given in level (standard) cup and spoon measures.

A set of "single capacity" measuring cups will enable you to measure all your dry ingredients quickly, easily, and accurately. (It is harder to measure fractions of a cup accurately when you use only a one cup measure.) We use one cup, half cup and quarter cup measures.

All the dry ingredients you measure should fill the measures, but should not be heaped up above the rim. The only ingredient which is PRESSED into a measure is brown sugar. It should hold its shape like a sandcastle when it is turned out of its measure.

Flour measurements are especially important when you are baking. Too much flour will make your baking dry and stodgy, and too little will make them spread too much. When you measure flour, first stir it with a fork or whisk in its original container. Spoon the stirred flour into your measure and level it off with the edge of a knife. NEVER bang or shake the measure to level off the flour in it, or it will compact again and you will finish up using more flour than intended.

We used to measure liquids in clear, graduated measuring cups, but we now find it more practical to use the same single capacity cups that we use for dry ingredients. You should fill the measuring cup so that it is brimming full. Don't carry a brimming full cup from one side of your kitchen to the other, or you will spill it, and your measuring will not be accurate!

If you get into the habit of measuring dry ingredients before you measure liquid ingredients, you will not have to wash and dry your measures before you finish measuring.

Because household spoons vary so much in size, we always use a set of metric measuring spoons. One tablespoon holds 15ml, and 1 teaspoon holds 5ml. (Australian measuring spoons hold 20ml, not 15ml. If you have Australian measuring spoons, use 3 teaspoon measures instead of the (larger) tablespoon. The Australian measuring teaspoon holds 5ml, as the New Zealand one does.)

Unless stated otherwise, don't use heaped spoon measures in any of these recipes, since a heaped spoon holds about twice as much as a level spoon. Incorrect amounts of baking powder, baking soda and salt can really spoil your muffins.

Making Great Slices

Slices are not hard to make – you don't need to be an experienced or wildly keen baker to make slices, squares, fingers and bars which will delight your family and friends – and give you a great deal of satisfaction!

What is a Slice?
A "Slice" is the general name we have given to a sweet mixture which is made in one large slab in a shallow pan. When firm, it is cut into pieces. These pieces (or slices) can be of any shape that suits you (i.e. squares, fingers or bars) and any of these names could equally well be used instead of "slice".

What Pans (or Tins)?
You don't need a huge range of pans (tins) to make our slices. Our most used pans are:
- an old 23cm square pan with a removable base and sides about 5cm high
- a rectangular pan measuring 18x28cm, available from many supermarkets and cheap chain stores (its outside measurements are bigger than this because of its rim)
- an expanding pan measuring about 16x20cm at its smallest and 20x29cm when it is fully expanded

If you multiply the length by the breadth of any pan, you get its area. The first two are close to being the same size, and the last one, when pushed in until it is about 20x26cm, is similar, too. Any of these could be used pretty much interchangeably for these recipes.

A slice made in a smaller pan will be deeper and will take longer to cook than the same slice in a larger pan, since it is depth that affects cooking time most. We like some slices deep, and others thin. You may feel differently, and use a smaller tin for a deeper slice, and a bigger one for a thinner mixture.

Preparing Pans
Different slices require different pan preparation. We always suggest the way we think is best in the individual recipes.

A few slices are robust enough to be put in a pan which has been coated with a non-stick spray, baked, turned out on a cooling rack, then turned over again, so the right side is up.

Others are best in a loose-bottomed pan or in a one-piece pan lined with baking paper which is big enough to grip easily, so the slice (on the paper) can be carefully lifted out, staying right-side up, and as flat as possible.

If you are making a slice which has a semi-liquid or liquid mixture poured over the raw or partly cooked base, before the whole thing is baked, there is always the possibility that some of the liquid may run under the base before it sets. This can make a real mess of the baking pan and cause problems when it comes to lifting out the cooked slice. We find that the best thing to do is to line the pan with a sheet of baking paper big enough to fold up all four sides. Make

definite fold marks outlining the base, then fold the corners as neatly as you can. You can use a metal paperclip to hold the corners in place if you like.

Although we use non-stick Teflon liners for cakes and biscuits (and much other cooking), we seldom use them for our slices, because of the temptation to cut on them and damage them.

How Many Pieces?
We have not specified the number of pieces made from many of our recipes, because we feel that this depends on personal choice.

From the one mixture you can choose to cut a few large "café style" pieces OR many smaller squares, rectangles or fingers (or even a mixture).

Whatever size pieces you cut, use a sharp knife and cut with care, or your slices will not look so good. We use our trusty small serrated knife, our serrated carving knife, and occasionally our heaviest large cook's knife. (See page 96 for details of our knives.) These knives are worth their weight in gold! Sometimes a hot wet knife will cut best, especially through icing. Because we are fussy, we sometimes trim off the edges before cutting our trimmed slab into even pieces. (The edge scraps are given to enthusiastic tasters!)

Food Processors
These are a great help and really speed up mixing, crumbing biscuits, etc. By all means use one if you have one.

Crumbly Bases
In many of our slice recipes we suggest pressing crumbly mixtures into (lined) pans to save time rolling the mixture out first. The easiest way to flatten the crumbly base mixture is to cover it with a piece of cling film, plastic, or another piece of baking paper and press it flat, using the back of a large spoon, or a fish slice, or a flat, plastic, bench scraper.

Oven Temperatures
We test-bake our muffins and slices in four ovens, and find that the times and temperatures differ in each. Use our suggested temperatures and times as a guide only, cooking until the centre feels almost as firm as the edges, and a skewer in the centre comes out clean. For example, if the temperature has not been hot enough to lightly brown your baking attractively when it is done, use a slightly higher temperature next time. To avoid over-cooking, always check the oven several times in the last five or so minutes.

Storage Times
The storage times given are very conservative. Refrigerated in tightly closed containers, many slices will keep for 2–3 weeks.

Index

Entries in red are low in saturated fat & cholesterol ♥

Knives by Mail Order

For about 20 years Alison has imported her favourite, very sharp kitchen knives from Switzerland. They keep their edges well, are easy to sharpen, a pleasure to use, and make excellent gifts.

VEGETABLE KNIFE $8.00

Ideal for cutting and peeling vegetables, these knives have a straight edged 85mm blade and black (dishwasher-proof) nylon handle. Each knife comes in an individual plastic sheath.

BONING/UTILITY KNIFE $9.50

Excellent for boning chicken and other meats, and/or for general kitchen duties. Featuring a 103mm blade that curves to a point and a dishwasher-proof, black nylon handle, each knife comes in a plastic sheath.

SERRATED KNIFE $9.50

These knives are unbelievably useful. They are perfect for cutting cooked meats, ripe fruit and vegetables, and slicing bread and baking. Treated carefully, these blades stay sharp for years. The serrated 110mm blade is rounded at the end with a black (dishwasher-proof) nylon handle and each knife comes in an individual plastic sheath.

THREE-PIECE SET $22.00

This three-piece set includes a vegetable knife, a serrated knife (as described above) and a right-handed potato peeler with a matching black handle, presented in a white plastic wallet.

GIFT BOXED KNIFE SET $44.00

This set contains five knives plus a matching right-handed potato peeler. There is a straight bladed vegetable knife and a serrated knife (as above), as well as a handy 85mm serrated blade vegetable knife, a small (85mm) utility knife with a pointed tip and a smaller (85mm) serrated knife. These elegantly presented sets make ideal gifts.

SERRATED CARVING KNIFE $28.50

This fabulous knife cuts beautifully and is a pleasure to use, it's ideal for carving or cutting fresh bread. The 21cm serrated blade does not require sharpening. Once again the knife has a black moulded, dishwasher safe handle and comes in a plastic sheath.

COOK'S KNIFE $35.00

An excellent all-purpose kitchen knife. With a well balanced 19cm wedge-shaped blade and a contoured black nylon handle, these knives make short work of slicing and chopping, and have come out on top of their class in several comparative tests. Each dishwasher-safe knife comes with its own plastic sheath.

STEEL $20.00

These steels have a 20cm 'blade' and measure 33cm in total. With its matching black handle the steel is an ideal companion for your own knives, or as a gift. Alison gets excellent results using these steels. N.B. Not for use with serrated knives.

PROBUS SPREADER/SCRAPER $7.50

After her knives, these are the most used tools in Alison's kitchen! With a comfortable plastic handle, metal shank and flexible plastic blade (suitable for use on non-stick surfaces), these are excellent for mixing muffin batters, stirring and scraping bowls, spreading icings, turning pikelets etc., etc....

NON-STICK TEFLON LINERS

Re-usable SureBrand Teflon liners are another essential kitchen item – they really help avoid the frustration of stuck-on baking, roasting or frying. Once you've used them, you'll wonder how you did without!

Round tin liner
(for 15-23cm tins) $6.50
(for 23-30cm tins) $9.50

Square tin liner
(for 15-23cm tins) $6.50
(for 23-30cm tins) $9.50

Ring tin liner
(for 23cm tins) $6.95

Baking sheet liner
(33x44cm) $13.95

All prices include GST. Prices current at time of publishing, subject to change without notice. Please add $5.00 post & packing to all orders (any number of items).

Make cheques payable to Alison Holst Mail Orders and post to: **Alison Holst Mail Orders
FREEPOST 124807
PO Box 17016
Wellington**

Or visit us at **www.holst.co.nz**